MW01165246

THE

ELISHA

CONCEPT

Vance L. Dash

This is the successor to the book the Lord had given to me to write in 1995, *"The Elijah Principal"*. 1995.

"And it came to pass, when they were come over, that Elijah said unto Elisha, Ask what I shall do for thee, before I be taken away from thee. And Elisha said, I pray thee, let a double portion of thy spirit be upon me.

2 Kings 2:9

PRESS

Copyright © 2004 by Vance L. Dash
Rhema Deliverance Center
3727—29 N. Smedley Street
Philadelphia, PA

The Elisha Concept
by Vance L. Dash

Printed in the United States of America

ISBN 1-594676-21-6

All rights reserved solely by the author. The author guarantees all contents are original and do not infringe Contents and/or cover may not be reproduced in whole or in part in any form without the express written consent of the author. The views expressed in this book are not necessarily those of the publisher.

Unless otherwise indicated, all Scripture quotations are from the King James Version of the Bible.

www.xulonpress.com

To My Favorite
Cousin In the
whole wide world
you are Special
and Blessed

Love always

Bishop

Founder & Pastor of
Rhema Deliverance Center

⋈

*D*r. Vance l. Dash, Sr. was born to the late Mr.
*William and Mrs. Barbara Dash. He is the
twin to Ms. Vanessa Dash, born five minutes after
his birth. He is the husband of Evangelist Vernell
Smith-Dash. He is also the father of three children,
Vance Loren Dash, Jr., Eboni Channel and Christian
Dior.*

*As a child, Dr. Dash felt the hand of the Lord on
his life. He attended church services regularly with
his family and friends at the Oak Grove Baptist
Church. He attended various Biblical and Theo-
logical Instates to aid him in his call: Faith Christian Bible Institute, Philadelphia Evangelistic Bible
College for Ministry and Maine Bible Institute when
he received his conferred Doctorate Degree.*

*He later joined the Gospel Tabernacle Pente-
costal Church, where he served as Youth Pastor for
the next three years. March 1982, Dr. Dash was
installed as Pastor at the South Baptist Church. Here*

he pastored and preached the Word of God until the Lord called him to establish a new work.

January 1987, First Church of Deliverance, now currently Rhema Deliverance Center, was established. August 1993, Pastor Dash was consecrated to the office of Bishop and as well appointed to the office of First Assistant Prelate to the Faith Tabernacle Outreach Ministries. July 2002, Bishop Dash received his Doctorate of Sacred Letters.

Dr. Dash is presently the Chief Apostle of Rhema Covenant Fellowship, which is comprised of various churches throughout the United States, Africa and India, for the purpose of covenant fellowship and covering.

God is greatly blessing Dr. Dash as well as the Rhema Deliverance Center, December 29th, 2002 Rhema Church moved into it's new church and multi-purpose facility—DEBT FREE—to God be the glory. Rhema also established a Community Outreach Center and ZOE Bible School. Dr. Dash is also the author of several books, tapes and videos, e.g., The Elijah Principals, Breaking Generational Curses, Ish and Isha, Strategies of Warfare, just to name a few. In June 200e3 the much awaited book "The Elisha Concept" was birthed into publication.

The Lord is continually showing himself mightily on our behalf, our latest endeavor is to pursue a door of utterance opened to us, National Media Ministry for the kingdom of God!

CONTENTS

PREFACE

—❦—

I give God all the glory and would like to thank Him for His goodness, His faithfulness and His kindness toward us, my family and my church family.

I would like to dedicate this book first of all, to my wife and children, who have been so patient with me and have shared me so much with the Body of Christ, with the local church as well as with the extended family of The Rhema Covenant Fellowship Churches International. Also to the faithful staff that assisted me here in the local assembly, but as well as abroad. I dedicate this book and this writing to you.

To all the Rhema covenant pastors, I thank God for your support, your prayers, your intercession and your confidence that you have in God and also in me, His servant. I believe that God has gifted me and anointed me in this in time to be a seed and a messenger, an oracle to the body of Christ, particularly to the Genesis Churches. I believe that this is the call of God on my life to minister and strengthen the Genesis churches that are birthing and establish-ing to encourage the shepherds, to instruct the *laity* in the fellowship as to how their relationship with their pastor is very important, and how that their prosperity spiritually as well as monetarily is greatly connected to their covenant relationship with their leader.

There are many that are members of local assem-blies but have not formed covenant with the shep-herds, the man or the women of God or both that God has placed to shepherd and lead them . I pray this teaching and the contents of this book, would minister to you the body of Christ, that it would unction a divine provoking through out the five-fold ministry that we might understand the relevance and significance of our relationship as it relates to our relationship with the men and women of God that God has placed over us to shepherd us.

Be blessed, be enlightened, be encouraged and share this truth in Jesus name, God bless.

Chapter 1

PROPHETICALLY AND DIVINELY CONNECTED

❧❧❧

As we read the word of God in II Chronicles 20:20, the scripture gives reference to the importance of the relationship between the prophet and the people. The word of the Lord reads in II Chronicles 20:20 *"And they rose early in the morning and went forth into the wilderness of Tekoa: and as they went forth, Jehoshaphat stood and said, Hear me, O Judah, and ye inhabitants of Jerusalem; Believe in the LORD your God, so shall ye be established; believe his prophets, so shall ye prosper."*

Now as we consider the text, the word of God teaches us that Jehoshaphat along with Judah went before their adversaries. As Jehoshaphat sought the face of the Lord and asked God for direction, the Lord gave him specific instruction. In verse 16 the Lord said to Jehoshaphat, *"To morrow go ye down against them: behold, they come up by the cliff of*

Ziz; and ye shall find them at the end of the brook, before the wilderness of Jeruel." Verse 17, *"Ye shall not need to fight in this battle: set yourselves, stand ye still, and see the salvation of the LORD with you O Judah and Jerusalem: fear not, nor be dismayed; tomorrow go out against them: for the LORD will be with you.*

God had given Jehoshaphat specific instructions how to come against or how to go into the camp of the enemy. The word of God teaches us that in verse 20, not only were they delivered from their adversaries because of the obedience of Jehoshaphat who was a king, but they   What do you mean? First of all, let us consider prosperity. All prosperity is not monetarily, utterly filthy lucre, money. Prosperity, I believe according to the Word of God, begins in the spirit of a man. God's criteria for prosperity is found in two places in John where the Lord spoke to Apostle John and said, *"Beloved, I wish above all things that thou mayest prosper and be in health, even as thy soul prospereth."* Now what John is saying under the inspiration of the Holy Ghost, He wants us to prosper naturally, materially, financially, but there must be a soul prosperity first. We must grow in the grace and knowledge of the Lord Jesus Christ according to Ephesians, Chapter 2. Then Proverbs 28:13 gives us another criterion for prosperity and that says, *"He that covereth his sins shall not prosper: but whoso confesseth and forsaketh them shall have mercy."*

So these are just two of many prerequisites according to the scripture for us to prosper, but then we cannot ignore this one that is very relevant. When the Lord said to Jehoshaphat, *"believe his prophets and so shall ye prosper."* I begin to dig and search to get greater clarity and understanding as to what the word of the Lord meant by *"believe in his prophet".*

The scripture took me to the word of God according to Matthew 10:41 for so long many of us have heard the scripture, *"He that receiveth a prophet in the name of a prophet shall receive a prophet's reward..."* Again this does not just refers to monetary gain, financial gain, money capital, but let us search the scriptures and find out what Jesus is really communicating to His people, to His disciples. Matthew 10:40 reads, *He that receiveth you receiveth me, and he that receiveth me receiveth him that sent me."* That is self explanatory. Jesus is saying that if you receive me, you receive the father because the father sent me and if anyone receives you the messenger of God, they are receiving Christ because they understand that you are the voice of God to the people. And that's what the prophet is, he or she is the voice of God, the oracle of God and the messenger of God to the people.

Mathew 10:41 reads *"He that receiveth a prophet in the name of a prophet shall receive a prophet's reward; and he that receiveth a righteous man in the name of a righteous man shall receive a righteous man's reward."* Verse 42, *"And whosoever shall give to drink unto one of these little ones a cup of cold water only in the name of a disciple, verily I say unto you, he shall in no wise lose his reward."*

As we look in the text let us contrast the two

scriptures. II Chronicles 20:20 again says if you believe His prophet, so shall you prosper, Matthew 10:41 says if you receive a prophet in the name of a prophet you shall receive a prophet's reward. The word *receive* in Matthew 10:41 and the word *believe* in II Chronicles 20:20 have the same connotation and they both mean this in the language of Jesus that He spoke (one of many). We understand that Jesus spoke *fluent Greek, Hebrew and Aramaic.* But in this particular text in Matthew 10:41, the text is in Greek, and when Jesus says that he that receiveth a prophet in the name, the Greek word is 'deoxomai' and it has a tri-fold meaning.

1) It means *accept*, he that accepts the prophet. What does it mean? Accept, simply that you accept the word, the message, or declaration of God that God is sending through prophet of prophetess. He that accepts the ministry, the anointing, the leadership, the instruction of the prophet. Remember in the five-fold ministry, the prophet is the pointer, the one that give instruction and direction to the body of Christ regarding the things of God. The prophet communicates the mind and the will of God regarding things present and things to come. In the book of Daniel, when we study prophecies of the prophet, the prophet always spoke of the time which refers to present tense and the times plural, which refers to the future tense. So that the prophet comes to bring confirmation, to speak of things present and also of things that have not yet come. So again the scripture, *he that accepts a prophet,* meaning he that accepts the word, the anointing, the ministry of the prophet.

2) The word *dexomai* means approves, he that approves a prophet. Approves means this, that you validate the ministry or the anointing of the man or the woman of God were not moving or vacillating into the sin on emulation. Which means that you esteem the creature more than the creator, or that you loose your identity and your personality, your individuality in the shadow of a prophet or a prophetess, no that's not the reference here. But approves means that you approve with what the man or woman of God speaks, preaches, teaches, declares, as long as it lines up with the Word of God, you approve them, you validate them.

Another form of approval is when you speak into the lives of other people regarding what the man or the woman has spoken that you confirm it to be truth and biblical, that's how we approve the prophet. You approve the prophet by encouraging other men or women of God to come and hear a word from the Lord through the man or woman of God, you validate them you cover them.

3) *Embrace,* he that embraces a prophet. Embrace means to cover, to be sensitive to, to love, to accept, that's another form of acceptance, he that embraces a prophet. Under embracing, I chose the word covering. It is important that we understand the necessity of covering the gifts of God.

In a later chapter we will discuss the importance of covering, but just for the sake of record and note; it is important that we embrace the prophet, protect the gift protect the anointing, to cover them in love as they follow Christ. Remember the words of Paul, he said, *"follow me as I follow Christ."* The Greek word is 'minetess,' which means to imitate me as I imitate Christ. So long as the prophet or the prophetess, their lives line up with the word of God , then we should embrace them, validate them before the people to let them know that this is a true man or woman of God.

The last definition of *dexomai* is to give ear to. Give ear to, means that we submit to their teaching. That we pay attention to the instruction of the prophet or the prophetess and to accept the message of the man or the woman of God; to embrace the truth that comes through them as we give ear to them. We don't hear the man or the woman, but we hear God through the man or the woman. If we have the Holy Ghost, the Holy Ghost will give us needed discernment to let us know whether this is the voice of God or the voice of man. So we must give ear, attention to the direction, instruction of the prophet as well.

Now that we have a clearer understanding on giving an ear or giving instruction to the prophet, as we have contrasted these two scriptures wanting you to understand the importance of relationship between the prophet and the laity or the membership. Let us go further in this. I want to talk about the benefits of being divinely connected to the prophet. The benefits of the prophet's reward or receiving, believing the prophet, there are three particular things that we teach regarding the benefits:

1.) *The prophetic declaration*—The prophetic declaration are the things that are spoken out of the mouth of the prophet. As we later look into II Kings,

Chapter 4, dealing with the prophetic declaration and things related to that, you will discover that God will anoint the man or the woman of God to speak things prophetically into your life by unction of the Holy Ghost, all because they have the ability to speak life or death, curses or blessings.

2.) *The designated things*, the things that are designated only for the prophet. There are certain blessings that God intended only for the prophet or the prophetess to walk in, certain blessings certain doors of utterance, certain window, certain gateways that only the prophet can have entry to.

3.) *Those things that are spoken out of the mouth of the prophet.* There are benefits to being divinely connected to the prophetic anointing receiving the prophet, believing the prophet, that God wants us to walk in and be *recipients of.*

They were also victors because they understood the relationship between the membership and the prophet. The first command of God was when you go down to the mountain, I want you to go there and set yourselves, don't fight because you won't have to fight in this battle. Also God gives them a command to worship.

Later on in the text as we read, the Lord commands them to call for the priest and the elders, call for the singers and the worshippers. Worship brought deliverance, but also the word of the prophet did. There is a mystery in this text, the mystery revealed is such that God said, "that if ye believe in the Lord your God, so shall ye be established." Let us understand that our establishment is solely based on our relationship with God, not based upon any exterior connection but solely based on our relationship with God.

To be established, to be rooted, to be grounded as we read in I Peter. Peter talks about being rooted as grounded in the Lord and being established. The word 'stable' comes out of the word establishment. One of the Greek terminologies is the word 'sterdzo' and what it simply means is to be enabled above your normal ability. The word 'sterdzo' comes from the word 'sterid' meaning power to operate above the normal and supernatural. So God will give us the ability as we establish in Him, to be, to move and operate above the norm or the supernatural. So our establishment is solely based upon our relationship with God, but notice the later clause of the verse the very last sentence *"believes his prophets and so shall ye prosper."* This indicates that our prosperity in a large part is attributed to our relationships with Gods prophets.

Chapter 2

THE ELISHA CONCEPT

❧❦❧

In Chapter 2, we are going to focus primarily on II Kings, Chapter 4. Here is where the text of the title of the book comes from the Elisha Concept. We understand that after *Elijah* the prophet died, Elisha became the head of the school of the prophets. Elisha was the pupil, the disciple, the spiritual son of *Elijah*. There is no indication in the Bible that Elisha was *Elijah's* biological son, but rather his spiritual son. Elisha being the successor to *Elijah*. As we notice in II Kings, Chapter 4, Elisha moving into the prophetic area of his ministry, and we entitled this the Elisha Concept.

In II Kings, Chapter 4 beginning at verse 8 through verse 11, the scripture reads, *"And it fell on a day that Elisha passed to Shunem, where was a great woman; and she constrained him to eat bread. And so it was, that as oft as he passed by, he turned in thither to eat bread. And she said unto her husband, Behold now I perceive that this is an holy man of God, which passeth by us continually. Let us make a little chamber, I pray thee, on the wall; and let us set for him there a bed and a table, and a stool, and a candlestick: and it shall be, when he cometh to us, that he shall turn in thither. And it fell on a day, that he came thither, and he turned into the chamber, and lay there.*

If you read the *Elijah Principle,* you'll understand that the same principle is *initiated* here in the Elisha Concept. How that this woman, who was classified or deemed a great woman, according to the commentary it says that the woman was renowned, that she was very well known, she was noble, she was rich, the Hebrew word 'gadol' mans that she was royalty. She had a renowned reputation and that she was rich, she was of royal *lineage.* The word of God says that this woman who was noble and rich and of great renown, that she perceived that there was something distinctive, something different about Elisha, and she said to her husband, "I perceive that he is a Holy man, a man of God, let us prepare for him a chamber."

According to the commentary, it says that the woman went though the expense of literally building something similar to what is called an upper room. In the Hebrew the word is 'aliyah' and this generally refers to an upper room in the eastern corner of the house. The woman literally had an upper room apartment built on to her house and according to the commentary it was a second story connected to a porch and the prophet gained access to it by a separate set of stairs that gave him private entry into his own quarters. This woman honored and recognized the anointing so in this man of God, that she and her husband went through the expense of building an apartment adjacent to their home, just so that when the man of God passed by, that he would have private quarters to rest and refresh himself, and I'm sure to get in the presence of the Lord whenever he came through the coast of *Shunem.*

The Bible says in Chapter 4:12, *And he said to Gehazi his servant, Call this Shunammite. And when he had called her, she stood before him."* Verse 13, *"And he said unto him, say now unto her, behold, thou has been careful for us with all this care:"* (In other words he said Gehazi tell the woman you have been so attentive to us, everything that we desired and needed you made sure that we had it, you went out of your way to make sure that we were comfortable and you spared nothing as it relates to finance or income to make sure that we were ministered to sufficiently), what is to be done for thee?

Wouldest thou be spoken for to the king, and give you a recommendation to let the king know that you are a woman of integrity and nobility, or to the captain of the host? Tell him of your kind deeds and your great works." She answered, "I dwell among mine own people." He said, "What then is to be done for her?" Gehazi answered, "Verily, she hath no child and her husband is old." In other words in verse 13 when the woman said I dwell among my own people, in the custom of the Bible time, it was considered a shame for a woman not to be able to have a male child to be the heir of the family to carry out the legacy of the family and the families name. She said, "I dwell among my own people and I'm barren, my would is desolate. I can't produce, I can't bear children and not only that but my husband I an old man."

It was customary also in Bible culture often for older men to marry younger women or even young girls from age 13 and up. She said, "My husband is old, not able to produce a child." In verse 15 Elijah said "Call her," and when he had called her, she stood in the door. Verse 16, and he said, "About this season, according to the time of life, thou shalt embrace a son." She replied, "Nay my lord, man of God, do not lie unto thine handmaid." Now the concept is she ministered to the prophet and as a result she was able to reap from her seed or sowing or her ministry to the prophet. The man of God said, "Woman of God because you ministered to me the very thing that you lack and desire I speak it into your life. I declare that according to the season of the time of life thou shall embrace a son." According to the Hebrew calendar in this time it consisted of a 10 month time frame. So the time of life for a baby as know it will be 9 months.

There are some who have addressed this text and preached from the subject *(By this time next year)*. But we all know that the process of conception, carrying and delivery, is not a 10-12 month period. So I choose rather to redirect the text and speak it as such that the prophet declared to her in nine months, not next year this time, but in nine months you shall conceive and bare a son.

The number 9 has great significance, the number 9 means new birth, it means finality closure, the closing out of the old and the entering in of the new. So the woman did conceive, deliver and bare a son in nine months because she was careful to minister to the needs of the man of God. Again, remember not being caught up in the man, but respecting the anointing that was on the man of God's life, and thus she had a right to receive or reap from the investment that she made.

"What do you mean investment Bishop Dash!" The investment was she sowed of her time, her substance and her goods into the anointing, and therefore she had a right to reap from the anointing. This is the Elisha concept, because the woman of God understood the importance of sowing into the life of the man of God or he woman of God.

I say this to you reader, know that every seed that you sow to the glory and honor of God and to the life of a man or woman of God, or to a ministry that is fruitful and productive, you are guaranteed a return. Paul said in Galatians 6:9, *"And let us not be weary in well doing: for in due season we shall reap, if we faint not."* And I tell you don't get weary, because of the seed that you have *sown.*

Some of you may question, "Well Pastor Dash, I've sown seeds and have sown into the lives of men and women of God only to find out that they were crooks, they were not genuine, they were not for real." God is going to honor your sincerity and your faith and bless you because you sewed out of obedience. But I caution you, make sure you sow on good ground, proper ground, Godly ground so that you can get a just *recompense of reward.*

As we look further into this chapter we move into the text and we understand that the women reaped the blessing as a result of sowing into the life of the prophet. But there is something else that I must bring to your attention that is very significant. I want to entitle the next portion of this chapter:

How to Put a Demand on the Anointing of the Prophet.

How do I put a demand on the prophet anointing? How do I reap where I have sown when it refers to the prophetic?

As we go back to the very beginning of II Kings, Chapter 4, here is a different story and it reads, *"Now there cried a certain woman of the wives of the sons of the prophets unto Elisha, saying, Thy servant, my husband is dead; and thou knowest that thy servant did fear the Lord: and the creditor is come to take unto him my two sons to be bondmen."*

Firstly let's understand the approach of the woman, when she approached the prophet. She came to the man of God, thy servant, who was my husband. Notice her humility, she did not come to him in arrogance saying, "Look man, my husband is dead, what are you going to do about it." She humbled herself and said, "Thy servant, who was my husband is dead and thou knowest that thy servant (again humbling herself again to the anointing and the man of God) did fear the Lord." In other words you knew, Elisha man of God, that thy servant my husband reverenced God, but not only did he reverence God, but he respected you and submitted to your authority, and the creditors come to take of my two sons to be bondmen.."

In biblical times if you had an outstanding debt and you were not able to pay the debt, your children then would be taken from you to pay off the debt and thusly deeded as bond servants. They would work until the debt was paid off. Notice the woman, and word of God says; *"And Elisha said unto her, What shall I do for thee? Tell me, what hast thou in the house?"* Now notice, had not the woman and her husband been in proper relationship with the man of God, she would have not had a right to put a demand on his anointing. She would not have had a right to say, "Look I have a right to reap from where I have sown. We submitted to your anointing, we have sown into your life prophet, we assisted you. We've given to you, we've done everything that was right as it refers to the relationship with the prophet, now I am coming to you. I've invested in this anointing, now I need to reap from it."

The word of God says that Elisha said in verse 2, *"What shall I do for thee? Tell me what hast thou in the house?"* And the woman said, *"Thine handmaid,* (still humility of the woman), *hath not any thing in the house, save a pot of oil."* The woman said, "I don't have anything just a little drop of oil." It wasn't a pot in the sense that we know a pot, a large container that may be able to hold anywhere from one to four gallons. But this pot the Hebrew word (acuwk), it is a flask or a tube that on the end it comes to a narrow end with a pointed end and a socket on the bottom, so the pot is really only a tube of oil. And the woman of God said, "That is all that I have in my house is a pot of oil," a tube of oil.

The prophet said, "OK, now I am going to speak into your life. You have a right to put a demand on my anointing." He said, "Go borrow thee vessels abroad of all thy neighbors, even empty vessels: borrow not a few." In other words, the man of God was saying don't limit the ability of God. Don't limit your harvest, don't limit your return. You've invested much so you have a right to reap much.

The text indicates that if the woman would have borrowed ten thousand vessels, I believe that God would have miraculously filled every one. But she limited her vision and her prosperity because she did not fully heed the word of the prophet, he said borrow not a few. And saints when investing in the anointing of God, sow into the house of God, sow into the work of God, the ministry, the word of God, the man or the woman of God, you have a right to put a demand on and reap from the anointing. And in verse 4 he said, *"And when thou art come in, thou shalt shut the door upon thee and upon thy sons, and shalt pour out into all those vessels, and thou shalt set aside that which is full."* And they began to do so.

Verse 5 says, *"So she went from him, and shut the door upon her and upon her sons, who brought vessels to her; and she poured out."* Verse 6, *"And it came to pass, when the vessels were full, that she said unto her son, Bring me yet a vessel. And he said unto here, There is not a vessel more, And the oil is stayed."* In other words because the woman limited the amount of vessels that she brought, and when she inquired of her sons to bring another vessel, her son said to her, *"There is not a vessel more and the oil is stayed."*

Hear this in the spirit, the 'oil is stayed,' represents that we have shut down the flow, we have shut down the anointing, we have shut down the ability of God because we did not fully heed the word of the prophet. We borrowed a few and the oil is stayed, the anointing has ceased, the overflow has shut up. Verse 7, *Then she came and told the man of God. And he said, Go, sell the oil, and pay thy debt, and live thou and thy children of the rest.*

My *admonition* to you, reader, is that you have a right to reap where you have sown, you have a right to reap from the anointing or the investment that you have made into the life of a man or woman of God, or the ministry.

Some readers may critically say that I am over rating the anointing of the prophet and that I am putting more *emphasis* on the man or woman and not God, no I'm not. God is a God of government and order and it is the divine order of God. God has always placed a set man or woman to govern the house. Later on we will discover the *significance* of that which is spoken out of the mouth of the prophet, when we study the life of Moses.

Chapter 3

PROPER COMMUNICATION TOWARDS LEADERSHIP

—※—

As we speak of the word communication, it is not in reference to verbal dialogue, but rather the word communicates from the Biblical sense. As we look into the word of God, there are two scriptures in particular that I would like to address.

The first scripture, in Galatians, Chapter 6, in Paul's letter and his *admonition to the church of* Galatia. Paul begins to write regarding the responsibility of the church toward the leader. Paul writes to them regarding their level of commitment. That it is not an option, but rather it is a responsibility, a mandate if you would, from God to properly communicate to leadership.

Let us look in the word of God. Galatians 6:6 reads as thus, *"Let him that is taught in the word communicate unto him that teacheth in all good things.* The communicate in this text is 'koineneo.'

What this refers to again is not conversation by way of verbal dialogue, words coming out of you mouth. But the word means to share, transfer, be a partaker of, distribute, give, and it really refers to the material support of the priest. This scripture is confirmed by Philippians 4:15.

As you read Philippians 4:15, Paul wrote to Phillippi, let us begin with verse 14. *"Notwithstanding ye have well done, that ye did communicate with my affliction.* The word here (affliction) is the Greek word 'thilipsis,' and it means, you communicated with my tribulation, my time of going through, my anguish, my trouble. In verse 15, Paul says, *"Now ye Philippians know also, that in the beginning of the gospel, when I departed from Macedonia, no church communicated with me as concerning giving and receiving, but ye only."* Paul is saying that when I left Macedonia ministering on a crusade mission, no church transferred, gave, ministered to, was sensitive to, assisted me in my need concerning giving and receiving, but ye Phillippi. You were the only church that ministered to me when I was in need, you gave to me and you ministered in giving and receiving.

In verse 16, it says, *"For even in Thessalonia ye sent once and again unto my necessity."* In other words, Paul said, "When I was on my crusade in Thessalonia, you sent to me not only one time, but you sent to me on a couple of occasions at lease, when I was in need." Notice his appeal to them in the same chapter, verse 17 he said, *"Not because I desire a gift: but I desire fruit that may abound to your account."* In other words, Paul is saying, "It is not that I want your gifts, or your money, or that I am greedy for *usury* or gain, but I want you to understand the principal that as you sow into the anointing and minister to my necessity, as I minister the gospel it's going to cause fruit to abound on your account. In other words, you are investing into your own life by sowing into the ministry, by helping me minister the word.

In reference, as we look in the book of Malachi when the Lord instructed the people under Malachi to tithe. In Malachi 3, when the Lord instructed, *"Bring ye all the tithes into the storehouse"*, which refers to the house of God or the storage place in the house of God, that there may be meat in mine house, the reference to the meat is ministry. In other words bring the tithe and the offering so that the tithe and offering can support the ministry. The word of God, the ministry that operates in the house of God. Paul says to them, "My inquiry or my request for you to do this is not with selfish intent, not with selfish ambition. My motives are not selfish, but I want you to learn to invest in the anointing, and invest in the word of God so that you can reap from this investment.

Philippians 4:14, I desire fruit that may abound to your account, so that you can be blessed. Notice Paul's statement in verse 18, he says to Phillippi in encouraging them. *"But I have all, and abound: I am full, having received of Epaphroditus the things which were sent from you, an odour of a sweet smell, a sacrifice acceptable, well pleasing to God."*

Let's dissect this verse, notice he said, "I have all

and abound," in other words, because you have properly communicated to the leader, he says, "I don't have need of anything, all of my needs are met." And to you the reader, I say that it is very vital and important that we understand the leadership should be freed up from the cares of this life and the things of this world.

What do you mean Bishop Dash? What I mean is this. It is very distracting to a man or a woman of God when they have to be worried about how am I going to pay my light bill; how am I going to keep my car running; how am I going to pay my mortgage. When they are distracted by the cares of this life and the things of this world it hinders them. It prohibits them from hearing from God clearly, it becomes a distraction, an interference and a hindrance. So Paul is saying because of you Phillippi being sensitive to my needs I have all, I abound and I am full. In other words, I don't need anything because you were sensitive and you understand the importance of keeping the man or the woman of God care free from material and monetary things.

When we keep the man or woman of God free from material and monitory things, they can pray without distractions, they can hear from God clearly, they can lay on the alter on our behalf and get fresh Rhema, revelation, instruction, words from the Lord. But we must make sure that they have all, and that they abound. He said that I am full, having received of Epaphroditus the things which were sent from you. And notice his words he said an odour of a sweet smell. The word there in the Greek is 'osme' and it means a pleasant aroma, an odour, a sweet smell.

When Paul says a sweet smell, another Greek word, that is pronounced 'eudia' and notice it has the same meaning of the first word (osme) but different *interpretation*. It means a sweet perfume, a pleasant scent, a wonderful aroma and if we would give attention to this, Paul said an odour of a sweet smell, a sacrifice that is expectable.

Keep in mind when you sow into the life of leadership, or sow into the ministry of the word, you have to see it as such. Not see it as, I'm giving to a man or I'm giving my money to a man or a woman, I'm sowing into the ministry of the word of God. Once you have sown your seed, whatever that man or woman does with that seed, you are not accountable or responsible because you did it as unto the Lord. The word of God says whatever you do, do it *heartily* as unto the Lord, not unto men. So keep in mind that you are doing this as unto the Lord to support the ministry of the word, for the saving of souls and the *edification* of the body of Christ.

So then, it becomes a sacrifice that is acceptable according to Philippians 4:18, one that is well pleasing to God. In other words, when you sow God is pleased, you're pleasing God literally. In verse 19, I want to give clarity to the scripture, that many believers are faithful in quoting in their time of necessity, *"my God shall supply all my needs according to His riches in glory by Christ Jesus."* This scripture is true, but before we eat the text let us chew the content.

The fortext implies, that this scripture is only

applicable, only applies to those that minister to the needs of the apostle, the man or woman of God. Paul said after you have done that which is right and given your gifts and supported the word, supported the ministry, supported the name or the woman of God, that it becomes a sacrifice acceptable to God. It is sweet odour in the nostrils of God, then you can say, *"My God shall supply all my needs according to his riches in glory by Christ Jesus."*

I hope that I didn't ruffle any feathers as you have read this, but often we take the scripture out of context and every believer is faithful to quote this scripture, but this scripture only applies to those that have been sensitive to the ministry of the word, the voice of God that God uses. The set man or woman, when you sow to them, God promises that He will supply your need.

So now that we have a clearer and a greater understanding of Paul's writings to the Phillippian church. Let us be encouraged to do that it is well pleasing in the sight of the Lord. In Paul's writing, he also wrote to the church of Corinth. I Corinthian 9:11, Paul says to them, *"If we have sown unto you spiritual things, is it a great thing if we shall reap your carnal things?"* Verse 12, *"If others be partakers of this power over you, are not we rather? Nevertheless, we have not used this power;"* In other words, we have not abused you, we have suffered all things lest we should not hinder the Gospel, we have done without some things. Paul said we lacked because we didn't want you to think it was just about money.

But in verse 13 he makes it clearer. *"Do you not*

know that they which minister about holy things live of the things of the temple? And they which wait at the altar are partakers with the altar?" In other words, if we minister to the things of the temple, we serve at the temple, we committed our lives to the ministry, should we not be partakers of the same.

Verse 14 says, *"Even so hath the Lord ordained that they which preach the gospel should live of the gospel."* So here again, the word of God is being confirmed as it relates to our responsibility in receiving and giving and supporting the ministry of the word.

Let us learn to properly communicate (Koineneo) to men and women in the position of authority. Some of you may say "Bishop Dash, well how do we know where to sow, or what ground to sow on. How do we know if it's good ground or proper ground?" I sincerely believe that as you pray and seek the face of the Lord, that the Holy Ghost will give you wisdom, knowledge, and the wisdom of God to know where you should sow, whether it is proper ground, good ground or not. You will be governed and lead by the Holy Spirit as long as you allow Him to lead you in helping make right decisions; making Godly decisions and doing the things that will be beneficial and profitable for you to do as it relates to giving. So be encouraged as you endeavor to do those things which are right. Seek the Lord for direction, ask God to give you wisdom and speak to your heart regarding where you should sow and how you should sow. Ask Him if it is proper ground, good ground and I am certain if you seek the Lord and wait patiently that the Holy

Ghost will give clarity as to your seed, how you should sow it and where you should sow it.

As we continue in this study of the word of God, the title of this paragraph is *'The Heave Offering,'* God has a specific order, those of you who have read the 'Elijah Principal' that I wrote, you will understand that I teach there explicitly regarding the entitlement of the priest. But I want to go further here.

In the book of Numbers, Chapter 18, as God begins to establish the Levitical and the priesthood order according to the word of God. In Numbers 18:6 the Lord says, *"And I, behold, I have taken your brethren the Levitis from among the children of Israel; to you they are given as a gift for the Lord to do the service of the tabernacles of the congregation."*

Now notice that the Levites, the associate ministers or the assistants to the ministers are given as a gift. As I stated in the book, 'The Elijah Principal,' according to Ephesians 4:11, the five-fold ministry is a gift to the church. I want to confirm it with this Old Testament scripture (Verse 7). *Therefore thou and thy sons with thee shall keep your priest's office for every thing of the altar, and within the vail; and ye shall serve; I have given your priest's office unto you as a service of gift: and the stranger that cometh nigh shall be put to death."* In other words, God is saying, "I am giving the office of priest to be a gift to the congregation as well." The reference to (the stranger that cometh nigh) refers to those that come to interfere with or to mishandle the priestly office or anointing, will be subject to death under the mosaic law.

Thusly, we should be careful how we approach

and entreat the anointing. In Numbers 18:9 we read how God begins to give specific instructions as to the things that should be devoted or allocated to the priest. Verse 9, *"This shall be thine of the holy things, reserved from the fire: every oblation (every special sacrifice) of theirs, every meat offering of theirs, and every sin offering of theirs, and every trespass offering of theirs, which they shall render unto me, shall be most holy for thee and for thy sons."* In other words, the Lord says every thing that they bring to sacrifice to me, I'm going to set aside so that the priest and the Levites might receive it.

Verse 11, *"And this is thine; the heave offering of their gift, with all the wave offerings of the children of Israel: I have given them unto thee, and to thy sons and to thy daughters with thee; by a statute for ever: every one that is clean in thy house shall eat of it."* God says again very clearly, "I have given to you the pastor, the prophet, the priest of the heave offering.

Now the heave offering is that which is rendered up, that was set aside by God. The wave offering means that it is available only to the children of the priest. So the sons and the daughters of the priest, as you read in verse 11, they had rights to receive a certain portion of the wave offering that came from the heave offering. But only the male child of the priestly order could receive the heave offering.

Verse 12, *"All the best of the oil, and the best of the wine, and of the wheat, the firstfruits of them which they shall offer unto the LORD, them have I given thee."* (the priest and the Levite). And you will notice that the word of God says, "and the best of the oil, and all the best of the wine." Of course in the scripture the wine is referring to unfermented wine. It is not an intoxicating drink, but rather the fruit of the vine. So God says specifically, "I want the priest, my pastor, my prophet to have the best of the vine, the best of the oil." So I encourage you to read this with clarity and understand this is not man's order, this is God's order.

Verse 19, *"All the heave offerings of holy things, which the children of Israel offer unto the Lord, have I given thee,"* again referring to the priest, *and thy sons and thy daughters with thee, by a statute for ever: it is a covenant of salt for ever before the LORD unto thee and to thy seed with thee."* So now, we move into a different dimension of this teaching. It is not just the will of God for us to receive, the priest, the prophet of the five-fold ministry, to receive the heave offering, but it is an agreement.

A covenant is an agreement made between two or more parties. What God was saying here is that this is a covenant that I am implementing by law. Salt being scarce and of a precious value was used in every sacrifice, and God is saying, "I am making this a covenant of salt." Literally referring to sodomizing any invaluable covenant. In other words, saying just as salt is valuable in this time, in the Bible time and was very scarce. God was saying that I'm going to treat this covenant like I treat the salt covenant and it is going to be very invaluable. In other words you can't break this law, it is a law of God that is not to be broken and we should treat it like the value of salt which was very scarce in this time.

So let us understand that it is not only a responsibility, a requirement, it is a God covenant, that God made with the people of Israel for priest, for the five-fold ministry. So when we disobey this, we are also violating a covenant.

Verse 24, *"But the tithes of the children of Israel, which they offer as an heave offering unto the Lord, I have given to the Levites."* Now again the Levites are the associate ministers of the church to inherit; *"therefore I have said unto them. Among the children of Israel they shall have no inheritance."* In other words, that the children of Israel were not to be the recipient of the of the tithes but the Levites.

Verse 25, *"And the LORD spake unto Moses, saying,"* Verse 26, *"Thus speak unto the Levites, and say unto them, When ye take of the children of Israel the tithes which I have given you from them for your inheritance, then ye shall offer up an heave offering of it for the LORD , even a tenth part of the tithe.* In other words what ever you get, ministers of the temple you offer a tenth part up to the Lord. But remember according to verse 20, the tenth part that the Lord spoke unto Aaron not to receive, he said, "I will be your inheritance Aaron." In other words the reference is, Aaron, I am your inheritance and whatever is given to me will be shared with you because I am your inheritance.

Then the Lord said in verse 27, *"And this your heave offering shall be reckoned unto you, as though it were the corn of the threshing floor, and as the fullness of the winepress."* In other words, treat this offering just like you don't mind yielding or giving the corn or giving the fullness of the winepress. You shouldn't mind giving the tithe. Verse 28, *"Thus ye shall offer an heave offering unto the LORD of all your tithes, which ye receive of the children of Israel; and ye shall give thereof the LORD's heave offering to Aaron the priest.* Give the Lord's tenth to Aaron, the priest. That's who gets the tenth of the Lord's portion that's referred to in verse 20.

So here God again has an order. He says "Levites you are going to receive the portion that comes from Israel but then Levites, I want you to take your portion and give it the priest. Israel, the congregation tithes to the church and the Levites have a right to receive that tithe. The portion that the Levites get, they seed a tenth of that tithe back to the Lord and the Lord said, "Give my part of it to Aaron, who is my priest."

Verse 29, *Out of all your gifts ye shall offer every heave offering of the Lord, of all the best thereof,"* Notice the emphasis on the best. God doesn't want the leftovers, He wants the best. *"even the hallowed part thereof out of it."* Verse 30, *"Therefore, thou shall say unto them, When ye have heaved the best thereof from it, then it shall be counted unto the Levites as the increase of the threshing floor, and as the increase of the winepress.* Verse 31. *"And ye shall eat it in every place, ye and your households: for it is your reward for your service in the taberna-cle of the congregation."* God is saying this is how I bless my five-fold ministry, the priest, my leaders.

So again, as we understand the word of the Lord, God gives clear instruction to Aaron and to Moses.

Aaron give your tithe to me, you don't receive any, Moses you receive that portion. Moses you tithe unto Aaron, but the congregation tithes to the Levites.

I pray with the utmost sincerity that as you read this that it will speak revelation to your spirit and please, as I say again, perhaps in redundancy or repetition, it is not about a man or woman or giving money to a man or a woman, it is the order of God. It is the government of God and remember this is a covenant that God established that we should follow through with and pursue because it is the word of God and the word of God is right.

As we conclude this chapter regarding proper communication towards leadership and the laws of giving, I want to call your focus to II Chronicles 31:4:18. Here again is a confirmation regarding God's law as it relates to giving and ministering to the needs of the man or the woman of God, we want to entitle these paragraphs the Heap Offering.

The Heap Offering

The word of God reads, II Chronicles 31:4, *"Moreover he commanded the people that dwelt in Jerusalem to give the portion of the priests and the Levites, that they might be encouraged in the law of the LORD."* So we see this too, not only as a responsibility, as a covenant, but now as a way of encouragement. God said give this to the Levites and the priest, that they might be encouraged in the word of God. Verse 5, *"And as soon as the commandment came abroad, the children of Israel,"* (the members of the congregation, the church members) *"brought in abundance the firstfruits of corn, wine, and oil and honey and of all the increase of the field; and the tithe of all things brought they in abundantly."* The children of Israel, the members of the congregation, if you notice in verse 5, they responded quickly, as soon as the commandment came forth and they brought in abundance.

The Heap Offering refers to ministering of your substance. You may not always have monetary gifts, money to give. But they continually brought them food, fruit, honey, oil wine, meats. They brought of the sheep, and the oxen. In other words, they brought them chicken, steak, roasts, they did not only give them money but they gave them of the field.

They blessed the Lord, they gave God glory and thanks and worship and they blessed the people in Israel. The word of God says in verse 9, *"Then Hezekiah questioned with the priests and the Levites concerning the heaps."* Verse 10, *And Azariah, the chief priest of the house of Zadok answered him and said Since the people began to bring the offerings into the house of the Lord, we have had enough to eat, and have left plenty: for the Lord hath blessed his people; and that which is left is this great store."*

Do you understand it? He said since we began to obey God by bringing in to the storehouse to minister to the needs of the priests and the pastors, the Lord has blessed His people. Verse 10, the people are blessed and we have enough left to the point that we have a great storage of things left in abundance.

In verse 16, God says. *"Besides their genealogy,*

referring to the priests, *"the genealogy of males, from three years old and upward, even unto every one that entereth into the house of the Lord, his daily portion for their service in their charges according to their courses."* In other words, God says every one from three years and up, they were to receive a portion as well. Verse 17, *"Both to the genealogy of the priests by the house of their fathers, and the Levites from twenty years old and upward, in their charges by their courses;"*

Verse 18, *"And to the genealogy of all their little ones, their wives, and their sons, and their daughters, through all the congregation: for in their set office they sanctified themselves in holiness."* Verse 19, *"Also of the sons of Aaron the priests, which were in the fields of the suburbs of their cities, in every several city, the men that were expressed by name, to give portions to all the males among the priests, and to all that were reckoned by genealogies among the Levites."* Verse 20, *"And thus did Hezekiah throughout all Judah, and wrought that which was good and right and truth before the LORD his God."* Verse 21, *"And in every work that he began in the service of the house of God, and in law, and in the commandments, to seek his God he did it with all his heart, and prospered."*

In other words, God said, "I have an order, starting with the males that are three years old and up, that are sons of the priest and those twenty years old an up, that are sons of the Levites; that they would receive a portion of that which comes into the house of the Lord." But here again give special attention to verse 21. The Bible says, "In all that Hezekiah did, he did it with all of his heart and every work that he began in the service of the Lord, as it relates to ministering to the leaders." The word of God says that Hezekiah was blessed and he prospered because he did it with all of his heart.

Be encouraged as you render your gifts, your sacrifices, your seed, your heap offering, your heave offering unto the Lord. You render it unto the Lord and God says as you render unto me, that I will take it and I'll do what I want to do. We cannot dictate to God after rendering it as unto the Lord, what to do with it after we have given it unto the Lord. It is then our responsibility to say, " Lord I am giving this as unto you, your order, or your government. How it is to be distributed is not my care or my responsibility, but rather it is my responsibility to make sure that I have rendered it as unto you."

By doing this beloveth with the right attitude, doing it *heartily* and as unto the Lord, not unto men, as Paul told the Roman church then we'll receive our reward. But if we do it *grudgingly* or of necessity, then we have lost our reward and remember this, everyone does not have to know how you minister to your leaders. For the Bible says Jesus taught for what you do in secret, your Heavenly Father will reward you openly, and I prophetically declare unto you as you read this, that there is a miracle and a blessing because you did it as unto the Lord.

In the closing paragraphs many have asked the questions, "Bishop, who's responsibility is it to ensure, to oversee and to make sure that the pastors or the leaders are properly ministered to and cared for?" The reason the question has been asked, I have been often asked the question in counseling, "Should I assume the responsibility of initiating the care for the leaders and their families?" Some have felt that they shouldn't do it because they are related by way of *nepotism,* through blood, others because they have a close relationship with the pastors and or spouse, and they fear being labeled as a "brown noser." So the question remains, who or what parties are responsible for making sure that the pastors' needs and the families' needs are properly ministered to or met.

I have experienced in over twenty-five years of ministry, different methods and groups in local churches that were established for the sole purpose of ministering to the needs of the leadership. Commonly, in churches they are called 'pastors aid' or in some churches they are called 'pastoral care'. Other ministries have individuals that they call 'Ppa's' (pastors' personal assistants). Some are called 'shepherds care', the name is *irrelevant* but the purpose is very relevant. According to the word of God, and I'm going to show you who's responsibility it is to be the eyes and the ears to make sure that the leader's needs are being met.

In the book of Nehemiah 13:10-12, we address who is responsible for overseeing the care or the needs of leadership. In verse 10 Nehemiah says, *"And I perceived that the portions of the Levites had not been given them: for the Levites and the singers, that did the work, were fled every one to his field."* In other words, because they were not necessarily being taken care of they ran, and the field represents work. They ran back to *secular* jobs, because they weren't being ministered to properly by the ministry or being cared for. Verse 11, *"Then contended I with the rulers, and said, Why is the house of God forsaken? And I gathered them together and set them in their place."* "Then contended I with the rulers," Nehemiah said, "I called a meeting with the leaders and I said why is the house forsaken?" Notice how Nehemiah connects the provision for the priest with the house of God because they are one in the same. And he said, *"And I have gathered them together, and set them in their place."* In other words Nehemiah wanted accountability to see who it was that was neglecting their job attending to the oversight of meeting the needs of the priests, the pastors.

Verse 12 says, *"Then brought all Judah tithe of the corn and the new wine and the oil unto the treasuries."* So there must be a voice, a Joshua one to speak in behalf of Moses, regarding the necessity or the needs of the priesthood. So who is responsible? Technically the whole church is responsible for the care and meeting the needs of the leadership, but then there should be delegated individuals with delegated authority, or chosen individuals with delegated authority to be the voice to speak in behalf of the pastors, the Levities, the priest as it related to their necessity.

It must be someone who is sensitive to the needs of the leadership, someone who is not jealous, *envious,* that has a genuine heart burden and concern for the needs of the leadership and the family. This individual or persons must have a pure motive, genuine concern and also understand that this is the order of God, not an institution of man, but rather the government of God regarding provision for the prophet and the priest. Take note that this is a Biblical mandate, it is not optional, but rather it is a *prerequisite,* a requirement of God.

In verse 6 it says, *"And concerning the children of Israel and Judah, that dwelt in the cities of Judah, they also brought in the tithe of oxen,"* We people of color learn to love ox tails, "I say that in humor", and sheep. Why was the sheep brought in? For the fleecing of the sheep. They used the sheep's wool to make garments, clothing and coats and things of that nature. Those things were consecrated to the Lord, their God and they laid them in heaps. That's the heap offering, the offering of piles, where they piled up foods, goods and meats and sheep's fleece and wool to minister to the needs of the leader.

Verse 7 says, *"In the third month they began to lay the foundation of the heaps, and finished them in the seventh month."* Now, that is interesting to note, it says in the third month, for five months literally the translation says they gathered the heaps enough for the ministers and much more was left over according to my commentary. So when we understand this, in the third month they began to gather and for five months they gathered so that they could minister to the ministers and much more was left over. The indication here, in the contemporary church today, we call it harvest home or *pounding* the pastor. We see that it is very much biblical and scriptural that for five months they gathered and stored food, oil, wine, the wheat, honey, sheep, the oxen in abundance. At the end of that period, they took the heaps that they had gathered and gave them to the man of God, the priest.

In verse 8, if you would notice, it says, *"And when Hezekiah and the princes came and saw the heaps, they blessed the LORD, and his people Israel."* Notice this, they blessed the Lord.

Chapter 4

MURMURING AND COMPLAINING

-❈❈-

In the last chapter, I expressed to you from the word of God, from the scriptures, how that ministering to the needs or necessities of leaders is well pleasing. It pleases God also. We showed you how that in Hezekiah's reign, it brought favor and blessing upon the people. Therefore, we must safeguard ourselves in light of this from the spirit of murmuring and complaining.

Remember the word of God says in the book of Psalms, *Let the word of God be true and every man be a liar."* Even when the word of God does not comply with our personal beliefs, philosophies and theories. Jesus told his disciples, *"We make the word of God of none effect, we rather obey the traditions of men."*

In my early years of pastoring, I will never forget, one of the leaders that God had raised up in the church to be a voice of Joshua, in my behalf spoke to the congregation, a very small congregation of not even 100 members. He spoke to the leadership at large regarding being sensitive to the needs of the leader, of course, which was myself. One of the leaders in reply, responded, well if Pastor Dash needs this, that and the other, let him get a job, let him go to work like the rest of us. Sadly, but true, it only exhibited her lack of understanding regarding ministry. Anyone involved in ministry knows that ministry is a 24-hour a day job, 7 days a week.

Unlike those who are employed in the corporate or secular world, that work 8 to 9 hours a day, she really did not understand the relevance or the commitment, the time frame, the responsibility that ministry entails. She and a few others began to murmur and complain about the church's obligation and just basic necessities. Assisting myself, at the time, I was not salaried. I was just receiving expenses and a stipend from the church and primarily, I was living by faith that the Lord would open doors for me to minister and speak a little. (Just before I began to travel extensively, God would touch the hearts of others to bless me.) However, I did take on employment in the construction industry, contracting and as you all know that kind of work is seasonal. This particular sister still did not agree in helping minister to some of the needs of Pastor Dash in the off seasons or the slow seasons of my employment. I would not allow myself to become angry with or embittered against this individual or the others that were in agreement with her. But I began to pray earnestly and intercede that God would open up the eyes of their understanding and as well, that the Lord would raise up others that would be sensitive to the needs and as well, implement them in the church. (And as well from a biblical prospective.)

The book 'The Elijah Principle', this book that you are presently reading, 'The Elisha Concept' and a teaching that I have literally done across the country in the last seven years, these two books and this teaching are birthed out of a lot of personal experience, not only personal experience, but out of twenty years of pastoring. I've had to encourage other leaders and by the leading of the Holy Ghost, minister to some of their leadership, regarding their biblical responsibility. I take time to share this personal testimony with you in part to encourage you to safeguard your spirit and yourself against murmuring and complaining.

We must understand the order of anointing. God never anointed from the feet up, but always from the head down. Which means the anointing, the oil, which also brings favor and increase, doesn't run from the feet up, it runs from the head down. It matriculates, as I expressed in the 'Elijah Principle' book, flows downward. In order for you to walk in greater degree level of blessing, you must get under the flow, under the anointing in order for you to be blessed.

God's method or God's system of blessing is that we insure and push the leaders, those in front of us, to the place of blessing in accordance to the word of God. If we are under that same anointing, whatever the leaders anointing is, then certainly if we are following them, then we will walk in the same blessings that God has predestined for them. Why? Simply because we are under a like anointing, the same anointing.

Let us be careful. In the book of Numbers, Chapter 12, as we began to share the danger of how we must caution ourselves against murmuring and complaining. As we look in the word of God, we began to see a series of events that had taken place during the reign of Moses, God's law giver, God's prophet to Israel .

In Numbers, Chapter 12:1 and 2 we read the word of God says, *"And Miriam and Aaron spake against Moses because of the Ethiopian woman whom he had married: for he had married an Ethiopian woman. And they said, Hath the LORD indeed spoken only by Moses? Hath he not spoken also by us? And the LORD heard it."*

First of all, what we must keep in mind is that it was against the laws of Israel to marry outside of your race and Moses married an Ethiopian woman, which was of African decent. Anyone outside of Judaism was considered unclean, so they began to look on Moses' wife as an unclean woman. How could this prophet marry an unclean woman? I chose to believe that because Moses was a man that feared God and walked with God, that he sought the face of the Lord and asked God for wisdom and direction in his decision whether he should marry this woman or not. The word of God says that *"he married an Ethiopian woman,"* one of color, verse two *"and they,"* referring to Miriam and Aaron said, *"said hath the LORD indeed spoken only by Moses?"* In other words, they began to question his ability to hear from God and they sarcastically said, "Is Moses the only one that God is speaking by," and they said, "Has he not also spoken by us?"

In the up-coming chapters, I am going to give you some information, and in your reading you will discover the importance of understanding the spirit of the leader, as well how God speaks and to whom He speaks to. Yes, God does speak to the Laity and the membership, but there is a different relationship between God and the people and that of God and the leader. Remember the word of God as we studied, it says Moses knew His ways, Israel only knew His acts.

In order to know a person's ways you must get into their mind. Moses had tapped into the mind of God and he understood the ways of God. Now the word of God says they challenged Moses and question him, hasn't the Lord spoken to us too? Yes God does, but in later chapters we will deal with the order of God speaking. But notice at the end of verse 2, the word of God said, *"And the LORD heard it."* Now beloved, we must caution ourselves and be careful what we speak, how we speak and what we say. It is very noteworthy as you notice how God heard the remark or the comment that they made against his manservant Moses. We must be careful what we speak.

I Timothy, Chapter 5 tells us clearly to *"rebuke not an elder."* An elder means one in leadership, not necessarily a preacher. An elder is normally one of the ruling persons in a governing body for a church. The scripture also says neither receive an accusation against one of them. So you're not only guilty when you make remarks, but you're guilty when you sit in the midst of those that comment and listen or receive it.

The proper thing to do is get out of their company and tell them that you chose not to discuss what is being discussed. Because whether you believe it or not, you invoke the displeasure and the wrath of God when we speak against the set man or woman that God has placed over us and in fact if they are wrong God always has a method of discipline for the His leaders. He always used the prophet to deal with the king or the leader. God will always send a man or woman of God. Therefore, it is not your place, it is not my place, it is our place to strongly intercede and earnestly pray that the Holy Spirit would deal with them and minister to them.

Looking further into Numbers, Chapter 12, as we read verse 10. It says *"And the Cloud departed from off of the tabernacle; and behold Miriam became leprous."* And Miriam became leprous. She got the skin disease called leprosy and the Bible says she *"became leprous, white as snow and Aaron looked upon Miriam, and behold, she was leprous."* Some of you may question, why didn't God smote Aaron with leprosy?

In verse 11 it says, *"And Aaron said unto Moses, Alas, my lord, I beseech thee, lay not the sin upon us, wherein we have done foolishly, and wherein we have sinned."* In verse 11 Aaron repented. This is why the leprousy, the judgment of God, did not come upon him. But Aaron did for a while lose his anointing and priesthood. So when we sin, God may forgive us, but there is always a recompense or penalty.

In verse 12, Aaron said, *Let her not be as one dead, of whom the flesh is half consumed when he cometh out of his mother's womb."* In other words, don't let her countenance be like a baby that just came out of the womb with no coloration and no coloring.

In verse 13, we see the prayer of Moses, *"And Moses cried unto the LORD, saying, Heal her now, O God, I beseech thee."* Verse 14, *"And the LORD said unto Moses, If her father had put spit in her face, should she not be ashamed seven days? Let her be shut out from the camp seven days, and after that let her be received in again."* What a profound statement by God. When God says, *"If her father had not put spit in here face,"* that is a very profound statement and it causes you to wonder.

The commentary states that as Moses interceded for her when the Lord referred to God spitting in her face, he is talking about the face of bitterness and opposition to himself. But thank God, God is a God of mercy and because of Moses' prayer (the bible says Moses interceded and stood in the gap for Miriam). God did have mercy on her and her health was restored. That is the importance beloved of being in relationship with your leaders. As I said in the previous chapters, to have a covenant relationship with your leader, not just membership in their church, but to be in covenant with them. That doesn't mean that you have be very personal with each other, but it means you covenant with the anointing, with the vision, with the spirit of the man or woman of God. Covenant means agreement, mutual agreement. You are saying in covenant, I agree with this vision; I agree with this anointing; I agree with the ministry; I agree with what God is doing. So let us keep that in mind, the importance of covenant. Certainly I would like to say that this was the end of Miriam's and Aaron's shenanigans, but as we study the word of God, we find that's not so. The word of God teaches us again they murmured and they complained.

When we look in Numbers, Chapter 14, and we look at the word of God, the Bible teaches us that here again we see complaints and murmuring. Numbers, Chapter 14 and in verse 3, the word of God says, *And wherefore hath the LORD brought us unto this land, to fall by the sword, that our wives and our children should be a prey? were it not better for us to return into Egypt?"* Verse 4, *"And they said one to another, Let us make a captain, and let us return into Egypt."*

Mind you, this is the voice of the congregation of Israel, the people that began to rebel against the man of God. In other words, they said, " We would have been better off dying in Egypt instead of dying in the wilderness. Notice in verse 11, the scripture says, *"And the LORD said unto Moses, How long will this people provoke me? And how long will it be ere they believe me, for all the signs which I have shewed among them?"* Verse 12, *I will smite them with the pestilence, and disinherit them,"* In other words, the inheritance I gave to them, I am going to take it back, *"and will make of thee a greater nation and mightier than they."*

Now we see the seriousness of God as it related to his plan, his will and his relationship. We see how God esteems his set man. God was angry with the people because they rose up against the leader and He was ready to take their inheritance, ready to smite them with pestilence, with sickness and disease. Contrary to what some of you believe, they had spoken against God's anointing. The Lord said, "Moses I'm going to kill them all and raise up a greater and a mightier people then they."

Beloved of a truth, if we would be honest, most of us would have said, "Yes Lord, go ahead Jesus, please do it, kill them, get rid of them. Raise up another people because of our weariness of striving and contending with the same rebellious and stubborn people" But notice Moses' heart for the people and it is important to note that Moses was a God appointed leader. Moses means one drawn out, or one called out of the water, and you have to be one drawn out to lead God's people because you must have a heart for them.

Numbers 14:13, *"And Moses said unto the LORD, Then the Egyptians shall hear it (for thou broughtest up this people in thy might from among them;)"* Verse 14, *"And they will tell it to the inhabitants of this land: for they have heard that thou LORD art among this people, that thou LORD art seen face to face, and that thy could standeth over them, and that thou goest before them, by daytime in a*

pillar or a cloud, and in a pillar of fire by night."
Verse 15, *"Now if thou shalt kill all this people as one man, then the nations which have heard the fame of thee will speak, saying,"* Verse 16, *"Because the LORD was not able to bring this people into the land which he sware unto them, therefore he hath slain them in the wilderness."* Verse 17, *"And now, I beseech thee, let the power of my LORD be great, according as thou hast spoken, saying,"* Verse 18, *"The LORD is longsuffering, and of great mercy, forgiving iniquity and transgression, and by no means clearing the guilty, visiting the iniquity of the fathers upon the children unto the third and fourth generation."* Verse 19, *"Pardon, I beseech thee, the iniquity of this people according unto the greatness of thy mercy, and as thou hast forgiven this people, from Egypt even until now."* Verse 20, *"And the LORD said, I have pardoned according to thy word:"*

Two things I would like to emphasize, number 1, Moses went to the Lord on behalf of the people. The intercession of your leader is very important, because in many cases it will change God's mind regarding you. Often as I minister throughout the country and teach out of the writings that God has given me, I often call the members to repentance, to personally repent to their leaders for things spoken, things they said against them. Why? To get them from under the curse because number 2, God is angry when we speak against leadership and when we raise up coups and groups to come against leadership. God is not pleased, he is vexed, he is displeased.

So notice, Moses interceded and said, "Lord if

you kill this people, then the Egyptians and the heathen nations that know that you delivered us from Egypt, and said that their God is God, He is a great God, they are going to turn around and say, I guest their God is not able to deliver them and He's not able to bring them out. He doesn't have the power." Look at the wisdom of Moses. Look at his love for the people. That is why many times, often you all say pastor, "If I was you, I don't know how you do it, I would put them out, I wouldn't keep putting up with them, I wouldn't keep forgiving them." That's because you don't have a shepherd's heart.

A shepherd has the ability to know his enemies in the camp, still forgive them, and still love them. I sadly submit to you that there are many under my pastor that have spoken negative derogatory things against me and against my wife, yet I still have to love them, pray for them, minister to them. Vengeance is the Lords, it's not mine, but one thing that is certain, if they don't repent first to God and then secondly to my wife and I then the curse of whatever, poverty, sickness, disease, generational curses, family curses, it won't be lifted until they humble themselves and repent. And I trust that you reader as you read this, that if there is anything in you heart between you and a leader, whether it is your current leader or past leader, get it right with God. They are not worth you missing the blessing the favor and choice blessings of God.

Moses prayed and asked the Lord, he said, "I beseech you, I beg you, I employ you Lord," in verse 19, "remove the iniquity, pardon them,". And notice in verse 20 the Lord said, "I have pardoned only because you asked. I pardoned, Moses, only because of your word." That is a very profound statement. God said to Moses, "I love you so much and I think so much of you that I will forgive the people for your sake." Thank God for the mercies of God. Thank God that God puts His spirit and puts His heart in the leaders so that men and women that have a heart after the God not being governed by their own spirit can be loving enough and caring enough to forgive. And as leaders, we must exhibit forgiveness and remember we can't be forgiven until we learn to forgive.

The word of God said be careful lest the root of bitterness spring up in you. The word bitter is the Greek word 'pilkria' and it means venomous poison. If we allow venomous poison to get in our spirit, it will affect our physical man as well as our spirit man. It will also prohibit and hinder the greater work that God would do in our life. So let us not be bitter, neither murmurers or complainers.

Again, we see in the work of God where the people in redundancy again rebelled in verse 41 of the same chapter, *"And Moses said, Wherefore now do ye transgress the commandment of the LORD? But it shall not prosper."* For the people again began to rebel. Verse 44 says, *"But they presumed to go up unto the hill top: nevertheless the ark of the covenant of the LORD, and Moses, departed not out of the camp.* Verse 45, *"Then the Amalekites came down, and the Canaanites which dwelt in that hill, and smote them, and discomfited them, even unto Hormah.*

What does this mean when we get out of the will of God, and when we rebel against the plan of God, the will of God and his leaders? God will allow our enemies to consume us. Whatever your enemies are: your job, people that want to see your demise and your failure, you going down, whatever your enemies are, let us not be found, let this be not so named among us that the enemy will use us to speak against the will of God and the leader of God. Remember Jesus is the chief shepherd, but the men and women that God has placed over you are your under shepherds. They are the voice of God to you, so when we rebel against what God is speaking through them, we actually are in rebellion against God and it is a form of witchcraft when you try to persuade others to develop a coup, to be in rebellion with you.

I teach at Rhema that the five-fold ministry is very important. When James said humble yourself under the mighty hand of God, he wasn't referring to a physical hand. God doesn't have a physical hand, for God is a spirit (John 4:24). But when he said humble yourself under the mighty hand of God, he was referring to the five-fold ministry, the apostle, the prophet, the pastor, the teacher and the evangelist. The five-fold gifting is the hand of God. In other words, submit yourself to God's authority, and I say again to you, if a man or woman of God is proven to be in error they are not following the word of God. Their lives are not lined up to the word of God. Then you are right, you are not obligated to follow them and submit to their leadership. Even if you know that they are wrong and you prove that they are wrong, it's still not wise to come up against them. It's better to humble yourself and leave that ministry. Get from under that covering so that you won't bring a greater judgment against yourself

Later we will discover how even Saul had lost his anointing, and David's' armour bearer went and slew Saul. David was displeased and so was God. David asked the question, "Weren't you afraid to touch God's anointing. Notice Saul had lost his anointing so we must be careful how we entreat the anointing

In Chapter 16 we look and we notice the word of the Lord, the Bible says that Korah, one of the leaders that came out of Egypt, often sought to discourage the people and not only Korah, but he had associates, one by the name of Dathan and one by the name of Abiram. These were those that came against Moses and began to say negative things, and began to speak against God's plan or the purpose of God for Moses. In verse 19 of Chapter 16 it says, *"And Korah gathered all the congregation against them unto the door of the tabernacle of the congregation: and the glory of the LORD appeared unto all the congregation."* Verse 20, *"And the LORD spake unto Moses and unto Aaron, saying,"* Verse 21, *"Separate yourselves from among this congregation, that I may consume them in a moment."*

It is important that you need to separate yourself from anybody that's speaking negative against the vision, against the leaders, against the plan of God, because God will consume them in a moment. Maybe not by fire, perhaps the earth won't open up and swallow them like it did in the book of Moses. But God has a way of consuming us that's invisible. He will remove your favor, shut down your blessing, afflict your body and I dare not prophesy dome to you, but I'm giving you what the word of God says.

Reading further, Verse 22, *"And they fell upon their faces, and said O God, the God of the spirits of all flesh, shall one man sin, and wilt thou be wroth with all the congregation?"* Verse 23, *"And the LORD spake unto Moses. saying,* Verse 24, *"Speak unto the congregation, saying, Get you up from about the tabernacle of Korah, Dathan, and Abiram.* Verse 25, *"And Moses rose up and went unto Dathan and Abiram; and the elders of Israel followed him."* Verse 26, *"And he spake unto the congregation, saying, Depart, I pray you, from the tents of these wicked men, and touch nothing of their's lest ye be consumed in all their sins."*

So association can bring a curse on you even in our judicial system. They teach that you are an accessory to the crime if you are found at the scene of the crime. You may not have made derogatory statements, neither made an accusations, but being present makes you an accessory to the crime. The word of God says after he admonishes them to separate themselves. And Moses spoke to them in verse 28, *"Hereby ye shall know that the LORD hath sent me to do all these works; for I have not done them of mine own mind."* In other words, I didn't do this because it was a good idea, but rather it was a God idea.

"If these men die," he says in verse 29, *the common death of all men, or if they be visited after*

the visitation of all men, then the LORD hath not sent me. In other words, if you see them die regular deaths, die of old age and if you see them die a common death, die of sickness and old age, then you'll know that's a sign that God didn't send me. *"But* (he says in verse 30) *if the LORD make a new thing, and the earth open her mouth, and swallow them up, with all that appertain unto them,* (in other words, everybody with them) *and they go down quick into the pit;* (notice the words of Moses, the word for pit is Hades, which is the place of departed spirits in hell) *then ye shall understand that these men have provoked the LORD."*

I must re-emphasize that they provoked God because they rose up against God's leader. Let us be careful, let us keep in mind the word of the Lord, to touch not His anointed and to do His prophets no harm.

In the book of Kings we read the danger of even mocking the man or the woman of God. Little boys who ran up to Elisha and mocked him and talked about him and gave reference to bald heads and shaven heads. Because they mocked the prophet, the word of God says that a bear had came and consumed them. God takes this very serious. And it is important that we take it serious as well, because it concerns God and what concerns God should concern us.

Let us caution ourselves not to be bitter. If there is something that we don't understand, let up pray or have enough integrity to ask for a forum or counseling session with the leader so that we get greater understanding. A lot of times, a lot of things are not understood and again, I reemphasize, because God speaks to the leadership differently then He speaks to the laity.

You heard Aaron and Miriam ask the question, "Does the Lord speak to us?" Yes He does. God speaks to the leader by His spirit and audibly. He speak to the laity by revelation through the preached word and by the Holy Ghost. But there is a different level or a different degree of communication. So let it not be so named among you, let it not be deemed or marked that you were one of the ones that was responsible for complaints.

Continuing to read in Numbers, Chapter 16, you will see the judgment of God, how the Lord spoke to Moses and commanded Moses and gave him instruction and I believe you will have a greater clarity. In verse 41, the word of God said, *"But on the morrow all the congregation of the children of Israel murmured against Moses and against Aaron, saying, Ye have killed the people of the LORD."* They refused to believe that it was the hand of God, and they accused Moses of killing the people. Verse 42, *"And it came to pass, when the congregation was gathered against Moses and against Aaron, that they looked toward the tabernacle of the congregation: and, behold the cloud covered it, and the glory of the LORD appeared.* Verse 43, *And Moses and Aaron came before the tabernacle of the congregation."* Verse 44, *"And the LORD spake unto Moses, saying,"* Verse 45, *"Get you up from among this congregation, that I may consume them as in a moment. And they fell upon their faces.*

So again, the people were provoked, again the people didn't believe that when the judgment of God came they accused it of not being God's judgment. But rather they made reference to it being the hand of Moses instead of the hand of God. The judgment of God comes beloved, certainly we will know whether it is God or man, there are certain things that man can not do and certain judgments that only come from God.

Yes, some of you may feel like them. Why did you bring us to the wilderness to die? We were better off in Egypt, at least there we had leaks and watermelon. We had wheat and barley, we had the comfort or the luxury at least of eating and resting though we were in slavery. I admit to you sometimes it is questionable the activity or the move of leadership. But in the next two chapters we are going to deal with, one is called 'The Spirit of the Leader' and the other one deals with sight and vision. They will help you better understand how and why God speaks in particular to the leadership as it relates to vision and sight.

Chapter 5

THE SPIRIT OF A LEADER

⊰∃⊱

In Chapter 5 we will be discussing the spirit of a leader. For scriptural reference, I Samuel, Chapter 14, verse 6. A very short passage of scripture, but this scripture was compacted and very much filled with a lot of revelation. I Samuel 14:6 reads: *"And Jonathan said to the young man that bare his armour, come, and let us go over unto the garrison of these uncircumcised: it may be that the LORD will work for us: for there is no restraint to the LORD to save by many or by few.* Verse 7, *"And his armourbearer said unto him, Do all that is in thine heart: turn thee; behold, I am with thee according to thy heart."* This is a very profound statement for his young armourbearer to make, that *'I am with you according to your heart'*. Often we don't have the sight of the leaders because the seeing is in the head.

As we examine I Corinthians, Chapter 12, when Paul began to write to the church regarding the order of the gifts. Paul said very many things that would challenge our intelligence. He began to talk about the different gifts and the categories of the gifts. If you will notice Paul says in I Corinthians 12:4&5 that *"Now there are diversities of gifts, but the same Spirit. And there are differences of administrations, but the same Lord."* There are diversities of operations, but it is the same God which worketh all in all. This confirms that there are different levels and different degrees of gifts.

In verse 8, Paul begins to give clarity of the gifts, he begins to speak of what we call the revelation gifts which is he said, *"For to one is given by the Spirit the word of wisdom; to another the word of knowledge by the same Spirit;"*

Then he began to speak on some of the power gifts in verse 9, *"To another faith by the same Spirit; to another the gifts of healing by the same Spirit;"* They all fall under the power gifts. Verse 10, *"To another the working of miracles;"* which falls under the power gifts. To another, prophecy, which is one of the vocal gifts, discerning the spirit to another, different kinds of tongues and interpretation of tongues , which are also vocal gifts. So everyone in the body of Christ may have distinct gifts.

In verse 12 it says, *"For as the body is one and hath many members, and all the members of that one body, being many, are one body: so also is Christ."* But I would that you notice as Paul begins to conclude the writing of this chapter, he begins to give deeper and further clarity on the gifts of the Spirit. He talks about the different parts of the body, the eyes, the hand and the foot. One cannot say that one is more honorable, because He's the eye and the others cannot say that he's greater because he's the head and such there of.

But I love Paul's description when he begins to talk about those gifts that are more significant and that we should not esteem one gift higher than the other because all the gifts or body parts are important to the operation and functioning of the body. That's where we get the word cooperate or the word cooperation. The suffix "co" means assist and "operate or operation" means a structure or government. So when we talk about cooperate or cooperation, it means to assist the operation or be in cooperation. Literally to cooperate with the mission or the assignment.

In verse 28 Paul says, *"And God hath set some in the church, first apostles, secondarily prophets, thirdly teachers, after the miracles, then gifts of healings,"* Gifts plural, meaning that there is more than one type of healing. 'helps,' now the word 'helps' is a Greek word that is pronounced antelipsis and it means to be a supporter to help to secure, to aid and assist. Often times we find in this capacity, stewards, deacons, armour bearers and other individuals that serve in these capacities.

Then he goes on to the "governments, diversities of tongues." Now the word 'government' is a Greek word, kurbenesis, and that word refers to the stirring or piloting or guiding a captain, director, a supervisor. Everybody does not have the piloting or the steering gift. The helps ministry cannot do what the governmental gifts does. The governmental gifts are the gifts that direct the ministry and vision. The helps ministry helps assist the governmental gifts.

The reason I take time to elaborate or give clarity on this subject matter will better help you to understand what we are addressing now in the text. What we are addressing in I Samuel 14:6 confirms what I just dissected or illuminated for you. *"And Jonathan said to the young man that bare his armour, Come, and let us go over into the garrison of these uncircumcised: it may be that the LORD will work for us: for there is no restraint to the LORD to save by many or by few."*

In other words, he is saying, "Look armourbearer, its just you and I, but come on, let's go over anyway and challenge the enemy because it's a good possibility, I believe God that He's going to work in our behalf." Notice the response of his armourbearer. If you would allow me to interpret, his armourbearer, said to him," Whatever you want to do, I'm with you, and I'm going to go wherever you go, I'm going to do whatever you do." First of all that takes a tremendous act of faith and confidence of the armourbearer to say what he did to Jonathan. This is why it is important to have the spirit of the leader.

I want you to notice that the eyes as we studied the human anatomy are in the head of the body, the ears are in the head of the body, the mouth is located in the head from a medical prospective. Several months ago, I did a teaching to the Rhema church regarding being receptive and open to the voice, will and mind of God. Those of you that are familiar with medical terminology, not that I am very well versed, but in my studies, we that have children often take our children to the ENT specialist, ear, nose and throat. The medical name for particular doctor is Oto-Rhnio-Laryn and Cology. Oto refers to hearing, Rhino refers to smelling, your senses of discernment and seeing. Laryn refers to the throat or the voice box, your sense of speaking.

One thing that is not associated with the Oto-Rhnio-Laryn Cologist is optometry. Optometry is the study of the eye As you so often hear me refer to the pupil, the cornea, the optic nerve and the retina. Those components of the eye that help create sight and vision. But as we connect those two together from the medical view point, it gives us a greater understanding of the importance of the head. There are certain function that the head can perform that the rest of the body cannot perform.

Again, I state that it takes nothing away from the other parts of the body, neither does it indicate that according to Apostle Paul in I Corinthians, Chapter 12, that the other parts of the body are insignificant or less significant. But what it does say is that each member must respect the other members because all of them are key important components to help the body operate efficiently.

All truth is parallel, so it is in the natural, it is in the spiritual. In leadership, there will be times when leaders will speak to give us instruction, admonition, challenges. We may not see like they see. They may speak things to us that don't calculate, compute, add up, or make sense; but remember you don't hear like they hear because you are not a head. You are a shoulder, perhaps an arm, a leg, a foot, a hand. They may speak things that we can't comprehend because again, we are not the mouth piece. Though, often you may not understand the leader, it is important that when you adopt the spirit of the leader or get the spirit of the leader, you will understand his or her or their spirit, though you may not have their sight, or their hearing.

What does it mean to have the spirit of the leader? To have the spirit of the leader means this, that I am so in tuned by the Holy Ghost to the anointing, the vision, the operation of God in the leader. I may not hear it or see it like they do, but I'm so in tuned to the God in them that when I pray, the Holy Ghost will give me to discern whether it is of God or not of God.

Jonathan's armourbearer no doubt, was not of the stature that Jonathan was, but when Jonathan spoke, the spirit of God in the armourbearer was in agreement with what Jonathan spoke. Evidently, it was of God. That is why it is important.

I John tells us to try the spirit, by the spirit so that we will know whether it is of God or not. But because the armourbearer knew the spirit of his leader, what he begins to do is move in obedience. He said, "Jonathan, whatever is in you heart to do, I believe in the God in you. I'm not worshipping the man, I don't worship Jonathan, but I believe, I trust the God in him."

Beloved, it is a fact, if we do not believe that God in the man or the woman that we should prayerfully consider why we are remaining under a certain covering or ministry. You cannot follow a leader that you don't believe in their vision, their ministry or their anointing, but you must believe in the vision of the leader.

You may ask, "Bishop Dash, how do I get the spirit of my leader?" First of all through prayer, asking God to make you sensitive to the man or the woman of God. Secondly, by knowing them. The word of God says *"know them that labour among you,"* I Peter, *"and that over you in the Lord."* The word 'know' comes from the word science, in other words, get to know their makeup, how they flow, move or operate. Require a science of them.

The word, Greek word 'gnosis' that's related to the word knowledge. Know them that labour among you. Get to know the spirit of your leader, how they operate, how they move, and one thing that's certain, if they make a decree, you will know if it is of God or not if it comes to past. We have to be careful not to constrict God to a time frame, not to say God if this is of you let it come to pass in five minutes, in five weeks or five months, sometimes not even five years. What is of God, I believe, if you have the Holy Ghost, the spirit of God in you, will bear witness with what the leaders have decreed or spoken.

I call to reference the book of Acts, Chapter 5. In the book of Acts, Chapter 5 when the apostle stood before the counsel that tried to accuse them of heresy and being sacrilegious. God used one by the name of Gamaliel to stand up and speak in behalf of the apostle. They were accused of being blasphemous and preaching things that were opposite and contrary to God. They were accused of being out of the will of God. But thank God, it is comforting to know that God will always raise up one to validate, to confirm, to speak in behalf of us when we know that we are doing that which is right or well pleasing in the sight of the Lord.

In Acts 5:25, the word of God says, *"Then came one and told them saying, Behold, the men whom ye put in prison are standing in the temple, and teaching the people."* Verse 26, *"Then went the captain with the officers, and brought them without violence: for they feared the people, lest they should have been stoned."* Now you all know the story and in your own time, I encourage you to read it. Verse 29, Peter begins to speak, *"Then Peter and the other apostles answered and said, We ought to obey God rather than men."* Skipping down to verse 33, *"When they heard that, they were cut to the heart,"* In other words when the counsel heard this 'they were cut to their heart,' they were angry. *"and they took counsel to slay them."* In other words, they said "Let's kill them."

In verse 34, the Bible says, *"Then stood there up one in the council, a Pharisee named Gamaliel, a doctor of the law,"* and Gamaliel spoke in their behalf. He had a good reputation among all the people and command to put the apostles forth a little space and said to them, "You men of Israel take heed to yourself of what ye intend to do touching these men." In other words, you may not understand them, you may not have revelation like they. You may not understand the gospel they preach, but if I was you, Gamaliel said, I would be careful as touching what is of God.

We must keep in mind the word of the Lord in Roman, Chapter 8. *"That who he did foreknow, God had a foreknowledge, he called and who he called he justified and whom he justified, he glorified."* Which simply means this, if He called you, He justified you. Which means He has made you right, He covers you and it also means God has your back. *"Whom he justified, he also glorified."* Glorified coming from the word glory, the Greek word for 'Kabod,' which means he puts His heaviness, His weight, He cloaks you like a coat with His glory.

And Paul said "Therefore if God is before us, who can stand against us." Who shall lay anything to the charge of God's elect. Gamaliel said, "If I were you, I won't touch them, I won't bother them, I won't mistreat them because of the possibility that this could be of God."

The word of God said, Acts 5:37, *"After this man rose up, Judas of Galilee in the days of taxing, and drew away much people after him: he also perished; and all even as many as obeyed him, were disbursed."* In other words, he is talking about all those that followed Judas in error in Galilee and rebelled against the work of God or the plan of God, they perished, they were lost and God was displeased. Now he says in verse 38, *"Refrain from these men, and let them alone: for if this counsel or this work be of men, it will come to nought:"* In other words, if this is not of God it's going to fall apart, it won't last another year.

But in verse 39 he says, *"But if it be of God, ye cannot overthrow it; lest haply ye be found even to fight against God."* In other words he was saying, "Look brothern, if it's of God I would be careful if I were you. I wouldn't try to overthrow it because if you do then you are considered what we called in the Greek a theomachos, which is a God fighter." Theomachos refers to God fighters and you don't want to be classified or deemed a God fighter. I say all that to say this, just as Jonathan's armourbearer was careful to study his spirit; to know him, according to science; to develop a covenant relationship with Jonathan; to adopt the spirit of the leader, we too must be careful and ask the Lord to give us discernment and wisdom. Often misunderstood, the word of God says in I Corinthians, that the natural man cannot discern or understand the things of God, neither can he know them because they are spiritually discerned, they are spiritually understood.

It is important to note that the fleshly, the carnal man cannot comprehend the things of the spirit of God because they are fleshly. In Jesus' dialogue with Nicodemus, St. John, Chapter 3, he said, *"Nicodemus, that which is born of the flesh is flesh and that which is born of the spirit is spirit."* In other word, He was telling him that flesh can comprehend flesh, but only spirit can comprehend spirit. You will only have the ability to comprehend and understand what is in the leader as you form a covenant with the leader though prayer. Ask God to give you discernment and also know them. Study them, study their flow, their anointing, how the operate, study their spirit and ask the Holy Ghost to give you relevant discernment and a truth. He will.

So we notice in the word of God in the Gospel according to Matthew, when Jesus had dialogued with Peter. Peter did not really understand Christ until he adopted His spirit. As you study the Gospels, you will note that not only did Jesus teach His disciples, but He breathed on them.

Two things happened when Jesus breathed on His disciples. First they received His spirit and they received a portion of the Holy Ghost. It is important to breath on those that are under you. No, I am not referring to standing in someone's face blowing breath out of your mouth. Neither do I dispute that, if that is the anointing or the operation of some leaders I respect that, but when I speak of breath, the word breath comes from the Greek word inspiration. 'Inspireal', when God breathed into man the breath of life in inspireal, He released His spirit into man. And that is what we must do, release the anointing of God, the Holy Ghost, in us into those that are co-laboring with us, for we are laborers together with God, according to I Corinthians, Chapter 1.

Jesus began to dialogue with Peter and Jesus said, *"Peter, who do men say that I am?"* Peter said, *"Some say that thou art Elijah resurrected, some say that thou are John the Baptist come back from the dead."* He said, *"Thank you for your account of what other people say that I am Peter."* Then He said, *"Peter, what is your revelation of me? The Holy Ghost quickened Peter and he said, thou art the Christ, (the cristos, the anointed one, the son of the living God."* Jesus replied, *"Blessed art thou Simon, son of Barjonah, for flesh and blood have not revealed this to you, but to my father which art in heaven."*

What is my point? My point is all sight is not with the eye, so even though you cannot see, as the five-fold gifts sees, the sight begins not out of the tunnel or out of the cavity that carries your pupil, but sight begins in your spirit. Which is another word for revelation or 'apocoluist,' which means unveiling. You can be physically blind and have sight. So, I say again all seeing is not with the eye because it was not revealed to Peter by the eye, but by the spirit.

When Jesus said, *"Blessed art thou Simon son of Barjonah, flesh and blood,"* in other words your eye didn't reveal that to you, but my Father, which is in Heaven, it was revealed to you by the Holy Ghost, by the Holy One. So as you seek to understand the anointing or those that carry the anointing or operate in the anointing you will not perceive, discern, detect nor understand everything in the realm of the natural. But it is a spiritual discernment, understanding, unfolding, unveiling.

Pray with me now. "Lord help me to understand and discern the spirit of God that is in the leader. Father give me the attitude of Jonathan's armour-bearer that I might respond, whatever is in your vision, your heart or your spirit to do I'll do it I'll do all that is in Thy heart, I am with thee according to Thy heart." That was the prayer of Jonathan's armourbearer.

Chapter 6

SIT AT THEIR FEET

❧

Presently, in the body of Christ, one of the problems that I have noticed, there is a lack of mentoring and pioneering. The reason Elisha became the great prophet he did was because Elijah mentored him. Samuel became the great prophet he did because Eli mentored him. Every one of us regardless of your status or your anointing, we need fathers, we need covering to help mentor, cultivate and develop the gift of God in us, which also brings us to the place of accountability.

I say it like this, every David needs a Nathan, every Moses needs a Jethro, every Timothy needs a Paul. We all need someone to speak into our lives. I will not compromise and speak to others biasly because of their emotional attachments to us. It is important that we learn to sit at the feet of great men and women of God. Proverbs 27:17 says, *"Iron sharpeneth iron; so a man sharpeneth the countenance of his friend."*

We need people in our lives that can sharpen us, that can help fine tune us and develop us. We need fathers and mothers in the kingdom of God that will help us to become what God has purposed and predestined that we become. If you notice in the gospel writings, each writer gave an account of the entry of Jesus ministry and His calling to the disciples. But one gospel writer of all that is distinctive is John. Matthew, Mark and Luke said, *"Come follow me,"* quoting the words of Jesus, *"and I will make you fishers of men."*

John said it differently, that gives it a whole other meaning, one word, John's account of Jesus said, *"Come follow me and I will make you become fishers of men."* That one word 'become' indicates process.

God bless one of the late great leaders in our city, the late Dr. Rev. Benjamin Smith, a great man of God, who fathered many across the nation. He had a popular belief saying, "You don't go to sleep a blunder and wake up a wonder," and it's true.

There is a necessary element and time, our perfect example, Jesus. Jesus went through a thirty year preparation for a three year ministry. Thirty years for a three year ministry. Sadly, in this fast paced society and this speedy technology, cyber matrix age that we live in, everybody wants instantaneous everything. They want instant anointing, they want instant wealth, instant success. But they are not willing to be teachable and sit at the feet of leaders.

I'll never forget in my early years in pastoring, a young man expressed to me a call to the ministry. Myself, being a young man, I expressed to him that I believed that there was necessary preparation, but I didn't doubt his call. I believed that he was called by God, but I believed that he needed to do several things. Foremost, he needed to stay before the Lord, seek the face of the Lord and consecrate his life even more. Second, look into some school of Biblical study, a Bible College, a school of Theology, that would help aid him and prepare him for his call.

Well, he did not adhere to my counsel. He left our ministry and went over to another church, where another pastor gladly accepted him. Within one or two months time, he allowed him to preach his initial message. Seven months from that, when I ran into him again, I saw him with a clergy collar on. I became greatly concerned, not with a judgmental spirit, but knowing that he had not fully developed or in the words of Paul 'come into maturity,' the full measure and stature of Jesus Christ, growing in the grace and in the knowledge of Jesus Christ.

According to Ephesians Chapter 2, verse 4, I saw potential, but I also recognized that he was undeveloped and not yet ready for the call. Paul said to the Corinthian Church in I Corinthians 4:14, *"I write not these things to shame you but as my beloved sons I warn you."* Verse 15, *"For though ye have ten thousand instructors in Christ, yet have ye not many fathers: for in Christ Jesus I have begotten you through the gospel."* Verse 16, *"Wherefore I beseech you be ye followers of me."* Earlier I expressed to you the word follower means to imitate, impersonate, the Greek work is 'mimettes' that means to literally imitate, impersonate the Christ in me, not become a clone of Paul, but to imitate the Christ you see in me. Paul says *"Wherefore I beseech you be ye followers of me.* Verse 17, *"For this cause have I sent unto you Timotheus, who is my beloved son, and faithful in the Lord, who shall bring you into remembrance of my ways which be in Christ, as I teach every where in the church.*

Paul was saying to them, he wanted to safeguard them against arrogance, pride, being puffed up, being unprepared, walking in their own knowledge, walking according to their will. His desire was that they come to maturity and allow God, through the Holy Spirit to develop them and to learn to be teachable; sit under men and women that are learned; that have Godly lives; that have good reputations; that have longevity in their ministries so that you can be taught, so that you can see them as Paul admonished Titus, *"as a pattern of good works."*

But in this upbeat society many just want to jump up and run. The old cliché states, "Some are called, some were sent, some just got up and went." We don't want to be classifies as such but rather we want to wait on our calling. Paul said, "Wait on your calling, make your election and your calling sure." One thing that is certain, man or woman of God, when you are called by God, the anointing and the gift of God in you will make room for you. At first we must learn to be teachable, 'iron sharpeneth iron.' Only those skilled in the word of God, that are anointed in prayer, that are rooted and grounded in the faith.

In I Peter we read God's desire for the church, for the body of Christ and this should be our pattern, that we be rooted and grounded, established and settled in the faith. It is important that we all come to a place of maturity that we might be rooted and grounded in him, that we might be established.

In I Peter, Chapter 5, verse 10, Paul says, *"But the God of all grace, who hath called us unto his eternal glory by Christ Jesus, after that ye have suffered,"* or went through a period or a duration of preparation and yes, with some suffering. Suffering will make you perfect. In other words, mature, the Greek word 'telleleo.' God wants to mature you, *"make you perfect, establish, strengthen, settle you."* in the faith, so we need establishment.

Again, the Greek word for establish is 'sterizo' which comes from the word 'sterode'. That implies that God wants to give us the ability above the natural ability to be strong and to be able to be effective in the kingdom of God, but not prematurely, not before our time. And we must be sober minded. In that same chapter Paul wrote, *"be sober, be vigilant."* We must learn to be sober and be vigilant.

The word sober comes from the Greek word 'nepho' and the word vigilant comes from the Greek word 'gregorreo' which means to be awake, watchful, and of a sound mind. He says it very simply, *"For your adversary the devil, for our adversary the devil, seeks whom he may devour,"* he is our defendant. His objective is to overwhelm us and to keep us from accomplishing the purpose of God. We must learn to be teachable. The word adversary is the word 'antikidos; in the Greek, meaning your opponent, you defendant. He wants to come and devour us, the translation here for devour, Paul says, *"he's like a roaring lion."* Your adversary the devil, as a roaring lion, seeking, walking about, seeing whom he may devour, that is the enemies job. The word devour is 'katapino' in the Greek, to gulf down, devour, swallow up. So we must be learned and matured and developed, learn to sit at the apostle's feet.

You remember in the book of Acts, when the apostles were doing great works and mighty works in the Lord and there was one, Simone, the sorcerer that saw the work of God through them that admired the work, that coveted the anointing and he desired to do the work of God. He desired to be anointed of God, but God had not anointed him.

First of all, he was not saved, secondly, he did not have the power of the Holy Ghost, thirdly, the anointing that he coveted, he saw the apostles operating in. However they suffered for it, they paid the price for that anointing and this man wanted to move in the same power.

Believe me there is a price to pay, so let us not be in a hurry to be overnight wonders, but let us learn to sit at the feet of the apostles and be accountable. I sincerely submit to you and I admit that had I sat a little longer under cleared and stronger leadership, that I would have been better prepared and a greater impact, a greater anointing of transference would have been placed in my life. Transference is important. Paul said, "stir up the gift in you Timothy that was given to you by the transference" or the laying on of hands.

We have to sit long enough under men and

women so that they can impart unto us by transference the gift of God. Many times we are impatient, we think that they are trying to hold us back or keep us down. But because of their wisdom and their discernment, they see often what we don't see. No man or woman can hold you down when it is God's timing or season for you to be released in ministry. But at the same time learn to respect the leaders wisdom. Many times we felt that we are ready, when in fact we are not. We don't want to be classified or categorized, according to I Timothy 3:6, as a novice. Which means one that is unlearned, immature, and not ready. We don't dispute that Barnibus and Paul had. Barnibus desired to take Luke with him on the missionary journey. Paul said to him, "No he is not ready," and according to the book of Acts, they disputed and argued to the point that the contention was so sharp between them that they departed and went different ways. The idea was not that Paul did not want to take this young disciple on the missionary journey. Paul understood that he was not ready, not mature, not developed yet. Later we read in the Epistles that Paul inquired, he said, *"Send unto me Luke, for he is prophetable unto me for the ministry."* In other words now he is ready, send unto me, he can be of assistance as we go to do the work of the Lord.

Let us not tread upon ground and in areas of ministry doing spiritual warfare with demonic entities thinking that we are ready when we are not. Learn to sit, become teachable, submit to the fathers and the mothers of the faith. Paul said, *"ye have many teachers,"* people that can give you the scripture, I Corinthians, Chapter 4, *"but yet have ye not many fathers,"* ones that are going to teach you properly, watch over your soul as well as your gift and your ministry, that will help develop you and cultivate you in maturity.

A perfect example of being a novice, or being unlearned, but more so in the things of God. In the book of Acts, 19:13 the scripture reads, *Then certain of the vagabond Jews,"* they practiced divination, casting out demons and things of that nature. But vagabond Jews, *exorcists, took upon them to call over them which had evil spirits the name of the Lord Jesus, saying, "We adjure you by Jesus whom Paul preacheth."* Verse 14, *"And there were seven sons of one Sceva, a Jew, and chief of the priests, which did so."* Sceva was a member of the Jewish counsel at Ephesus, and chief of the priest there. In verse 15 it says, *And the evil spirit answered and said, Jesus I know, and Paul I know; but who are ye?"* They were aware of Jesus, they were aware of Paul, but the evil spirit spoke back and said, "But who are you?" This again gives witness to the fact that we need to be taught, we should be teachable.

The ministry and the covering that you sit under are very, very important. The book of Genesis declares in 1:11 & 12, it reads that ever seed reproduces after it's own kind. Simply what the scriptures are referring to is that only orange seeds can produce oranges, apple seed produces apples, grape seeds produce grapes; you are what you eat and you are the product of your element or your environment. Thusly, it is equally important to associate yourself, to align yourself with whatever it is that you want to become in Christ, in the kingdom of God. Therefore it is very important that we give strict attention and be very prayerful as to our decision making process in ministry.

I teach this, whatever you want to become, you must associate yourself with. In the book of Proverbs the writer writes somewhere around the 21st chapter, "if the ruler in the house be wicked, then the servants will be wicked." Whatever anointing is on the house, the anointing will effect your person. Only hawks can produce hawks, and eagles can produce eagles. Therefore, it is important to align yourself with a like anointing.

Sadly, but true, many people are sitting in churches dying spiritually. Why? Because of nepotism, because of longevity, my great grand mom, my family has been a part of this church for five generations and they will stay and remain. They will leave their church and run over to another church just to get fed, but they will go back to a dead tabernacle. The unfair thing about it is this, we're not receiving some of us, what we need from the ministries we are sitting under, but then we go and pull on another man or woman of God, pull on their gift, pull on their anointing. But you will give your seed, your tithe, your offering, your support to the church where you are not growing.

I ask you this question as the lepers dialogued and conversed among each other in the book of Kings, *"Why sit ye there and die?"* If you are not sitting under an anointed, Christ centered, word filled, Holy

Ghost filled church, that operates apostolically, prophetically and under the divine unction of the spirit of God, then how can you become apostolic, spirit filled, anointed. Only anointing can produce anointing. Again, I quote to you Proverbs 27:17, *"Iron sharpeneth iron, so a man sharpeneth the countenance of his friend."* Ecclesiastes 10:1 is a very profound scripture, it says, *"Dead flies cause the ointment of the apothecary to send forth a stinking savour:"*

In the Arabic, in the eastern culture, they would create ointments and salves and perfumes. They would make them and they would be contained in a barrel or a bucket. If they didn't cover the barrel, the flies would gravitate to the ointment of perfume because of the aroma that it pertuded. Often times, they would get there and get stuck in the ointment because it was heavy in content, with a log of consistency, thickness and because they lacked the strength, they were not able to get out of the ointment.

The ointment represents your anointing and dead flies represent anything that would bring stench or dishonor or reproach to your anointing. So it is important to understand that dead flies will cause the anointing or the ointment to stink. You do not want to be associated with anything that is dead spiritually, so again I say "Why sit ye there and die?

Only eagles can breed eagles. If you know of a certainty that you have an eagle ministry, or a prophetic ministry God has called you to operate and move in deliverance. The Lord has anointed you to operated in the gifts and you are sitting under a ministry that does not believe in the gifts of anointing, they don't teach it, preach it or exhibit it, they don't move in signs and wonders, you are only prohibiting, hindering and delaying what God wants to do in and through you.

Only hawks can cultivate and raise up hawks, only eagles can raise and develop eagles, only apostles can nurture apostles. Prophets breed prophets. What are you saying? I am not telling you to jump up and leave your church. But what I am saying is this, as the head is, so is the people; as the priest is so are the people. And I know I too was in the mind frame, oh we are just going to stay here and intercede and keep praying, and praying. Prayer does work, but if the leader is not sensitive to the Holy Ghost, you can pray from now until next year this time. If they are not hearing the voice of God, you are just beating against the air. Whatever it is that God has put in your spirit or the Holy Ghost is developing you to become, remember what Jesus said, *"I will make you to become."* which indicates process. But you need a pioneer a mentor, a father a matriarch, a mother in the faith that's already there that can help develop you.

You know the old proverb, "Going there, can't tell, been there, how to get there". You need someone who has already experienced different spheres and dimensions and levels in the spirit that can help guide and coach you and teach you to hear the voice of the Lord as Eli did Samuel. Sit at the feet of anointed leadership, glean from them glean from their anointing. Observe the operation of the spirit of God through them, and God will through them, teach you.

Paul, the greatest apostle of the New Testament, who wrote 13 letters, birthed many sons, Titus, Timothy, Philemon, just to name a few. These sons that he wrote epistles to. He birthed them and raised them in the spirit. I Corinthians, Chapter 9, Paul said to the church, *"For the seal of mine apostleship are ye in the Lord. You are the evidence that I am an apostle, because I birthed you in the spirit, through travail, through suffering, through teaching."* Remember regardless of your anointing or how anointed you are, we all need mentoring, pioneering and we need covering. We are going to discuss the subject of what it means to be a covering in the next chapter.

Chapter 7

URIAH'S PERSUSION

T he name 'Uriah' means light of Jehovah. In II Samuel 11:6, the word of God says, *"And David sent to Joab, saying, Send me Uriah the Hittite. And Joab sent Uriah to David."* Verse 7, *"And when Uriah was come unto him, David demanded of him how Joab did, and how the people did, and how the war prospered."* Verse 8, *"And David said to Uriah, Go down to thy house, and wash thy feet. And Uriah departed out of the king's house, and there followed him a mess of meat from the king."* Verse 9, *"But Uriah slept at the door of the king's house with all the servants of his lord, and went not down to his house."* Verse 10, *"And when they had told David, saying Uriah went not down unto his house, David said unto Uriah, Calmest thou not from thy journey? Why then didst thou not go down unto thine house?"* Verse 11, *"And Uriah said unto David, The ark, and Israel, and Judah, abide in tents; and my lord Joab, and the servants of my lord, are encamped in the open fields; shall I then to into mine house, to eat and to drink, and to lie with my wife? As thou livest, and as thy soul liveth, I will not do this thing."*

First of all, what I would like to bring to your attention under the title of this chapter is Uriah's persuasion. The responsibility of the shepherd is to feed the sheep and to watch over the sheep. But then who watches over the shepherd, who covers the shepherd. I believe that God raises up men and women. First of all, they must be intercessors, having the ability to pray in the Holy Ghost and see in the spirit. Not judgmental, but intercessors.

The difference between and intercessor and a judge is, an intercessor pleads mercy, a judge pronounces judgment. It is virtually impossible to mark or deem yourself as an intercessor with a judgmental spirit, because then your interest conflict and there is a contradiction of purpose. You can not judge and plead mercy at the same time. So remember if you are an intercessor, you stand in the gap, you interceded. If you're a judge or one who gives judgment, then you pronounce judgment based upon the crime or the offense committed. Leaders need covering, they need men and women to watch over them. They need men and women with eyes that can see, that can perceive, that can discern the enemy when the enemy would come in.

Why is it important? Remember what Jesus said, *"That if the enemy can bind the strong man of the house, then he can bind the whole house."* The strong man represents the head of the house, naturally speaking that is the husband or the man of the house. Spiritually speaking, that is the oracle, the set man, the set woman, the voice of the house of God. That is why it is very important to have intercessors and coverings, Armour bearers to protect the gift of God, the anointing.

In the Elijah Principal, I wrote about David in I Samuel, how Abiashei protected and covered him and how Ishbebonob the son of the priest protected David from Abiashei. In this text, we see a similar situation, again the relevance and the importance of protecting the gift of God and being a covering. David had his men in the field fighting and at war. Joab came back to David and gave David a good report that they prospered in the war, in other words that they were winning.

Unfortunately, David's motives were impure. He coveted another man's wife, he aspired to take Bathsheba unto himself. Had David been in the field and at battle, like he should have been, perhaps this would not have happened. That's the danger of us being in the wrong place at the wrong time. Nevertheless, when David commanded Uriah to go down to his house, I would love to say that David's intents were pure because he wanted to give Uriah a day off, that wasn't the case.

David knew that he had sinned against God, by committing adultery and taking another man's wife, so instead he commissioned Uriah, who was a faithful servant. Uriah was a man of war and as well he protected Joab, also he served David the king. David's intent was to send Uriah to his house so he could be with his wife. As the scripture says, 'lie with his wife' and that way, the conception would be covered up. Uriah, which means light of Jehovah, was a committed soldier and armor bearer.

If you would notice the response of Uriah in verse 11 of Chapter 11, II Samuel, *"And Uriah said unto David, The ark, and Israel, and Judah, abide in tents; and my lord Joab and the servants of my lord are encamped in the open field; shall I then go to mine house, to eat and to drink, and to lie with my wife? As thou livest, and as thy soul liveth, I will not do this thing."* In other words, Uriah is saying, "Lord the ark of the covenant, the people of Israel and Judah, they are in jeopardy. They are sitting targets to the enemy and why should I be favored to the point that I should go home and lie in comfort, when the rest of these men and soldiers and armor bearers are at the post." That was Uriah's conviction, his persuasion.

Notice in verse 9 when David commanded Uriah to go home to be with his wife, Uriah was so committed to the cause and the vision, that Uriah slept at the door of the king's house. His conviction was that I am going to protect the king at all cost and I am going to cover the things that are of value and worth. And Uriah went not down to his house. Though David had wrong intentions and impure motives, Uriah the Hittite had the right intent. Firstly, he was focused, secondly he knew his objective, that he was responsible for protecting the gift, the anointing of God.

And I say to you reader, if God has anointed you

or placed you to be a covering or a protector to the gift, your first responsibility is to be a man or a woman of prayer. Secondly, you must be a man or a woman of warfare; know how to pray in the Holy Ghost, know how to do battle in the Spirit, to war in the Spirit. Throughout the scripture in the Old Testament, in particular, we discover how men and women, who were men and women of warfare, had their weapons of war and they covered and protected the king, the leader, the priest, the prophet, because they understood the importance of protecting the gift.

We too must understand the importance of protecting the gift of God, the anointing of God. Again, we are not eluding to the sin of emulation, where we begin to esteem the creature more than the creator, but rather we refer to the importance of recognizing that God holds us in part accountable or responsible for being coverings and protectors of the gifts that he has entrusted to the body of Christ. And as we protect the gifts and the anointing that God has entrusted to us then that will ensure that they will be available to minister to us and to serve us.

I teach on intercession, part of being a covering and being an intercessor, is being able to take the hits, the fiery darts. The Greek word for the fiery darts in I Peter is 'belos' and then we read about the fiery trials, but the fiery darts means darts that explode when they hit you. The enemy would to hit us; he would to hit the leaders in the kingdom with fiery darts. Sometimes as intercessors, we intercept the attack that was intended for our leaders, but don't be discouraged neither faint. Don't be discouraged because just as you intercepted darts, the attacks of the enemy, you will be a recipient and catch some of the blessings that are sent in the direction of the leaders that you are covering. So don't lose heart as you are protecting the gift of God and covering the gift of God.

Many of you know the story of Noah, how Noah in drunkenness and stupor in Genesis 9:1, the Lord had blessed Noah in the earth. Verse 1 says, *"And God blessed Noah and his sons, and said unto them, Be fruitful, and multiply, and replenish the earth."* This is the command God gave unto Noah, and after God had spoken unto him the Noahatic covenant and promised that the blessings of the Lord would come upon him. In verse 20, it says, *"And Noah began to be an husbandman, and he planted a vineyard:"* Verse 21, *"And he drank of the wine, and was drunken; and he was uncovered within his tent."* Noah was celebrating the blessings that God had given him. He planted a vineyard and of the vineyard, he made wine according to the scripture and he became drunk. The scripture says that Noah went in his tent and was drunken, but also he was naked, he was uncovered. Verse 22, *"And Ham, the father of Canaan, saw the nakedness of his father, and told his two brethren without."* Verse 23, *"And Shem and Japheth took a garment, and laid it upon both their shoulders, and went backward, and covered the nakedness of their father; and their faces were back, and they saw not their father's nakedness."*

This is a clear indication of the significance of being coverings to your leaders. Let me be the first to say to you, leaders are human, they are fleshly like you. I dare not give reference to the condoning of sin. Sin is sin, whether a leader commits sin or a lay member and God does not make exception, because you are a leader. What the body of Christ must learn to do is cover, not condone. What is the difference Bishop? How do I cover without condoning?

To cover someone is to recognize their faults, their shortcomings, and their weaknesses, and to speak the truth to them in love that they may grow up as Paul said the church of Ephesians. Tell them, "Brother, sister, you are wrong, that's not right, it is not of God, but I love God enough and I love you enough to pray and intercede for you. To fast with you if necessary until you get strengthened and gain victory in that area that you are struggling with." No his sons did not run around exposing him, telling everybody, look at what he did. He got drunk and he was laying in the tent naked, but rather they saw the necessity cover their father.

We too must be sensitive to our fathers in the faith, to our mothers in the faith. When a leader practices sin and has a life of sin, then yes you should pray for direction from the Lord, and be released from that covering. You don't need a sin covering, but there are times because men and women are frail and human and of flesh that they may fall or make a mistake. The difference between making mistakes, according to what Paul said in Roman is that because the law of sin lives within us we give occasion to sin. The difference is this, when you are living holy, you do not practice sin. Practice means a daily, weekly or whatever you chose to call it, reputation of an ungodly practice. For the Bible says in the book of James, *"he that practices sin is of the devil."* But in Galatians, Chapter 6, let us remember what the writer says, *"Brethren if a man be overtakin in a fall, ye which are spiritual, restore such a one with the spirit of meekness."* Paul said in another writing, *"Considering thy self also lest you also be tempted."*

No, we don't condone sin. All unrighteousness is sin and the wages or the penalty, the paycheck, and the compensation is death, spiritual death and eventually physical death. So we don't and we cannot justify sin, but we must learn to be restorers. Noah's sons did not condone his drunkenness, they realized the value of the gift, they understood that he was the father.

And many times beloved it is important for us to understand that before we take it upon ourselves to exploit and expose men and women of God, we need to pray about it first, seek the Lord, allow God to chastise them, to expose them. If their lives are ungodly then you seek the Lord as to which direction He would have you to go. Don't shipwreck the church, don't call yourself playing God, exposing the leader. That is not your place and you have to be careful lest a greater condemnation come upon you. God never called you to expose leadership, but to pray for them. So we see that they backed into the room backwards, not forwards, but these men backed in the room backwards as they noticed their father Noah's nakedness. And the word of God says, *"and their faces remained backwards."* In other words they wouldn't even turn around and look at Noah, but they covered him.

Keep this in mind beloveth, as you do unto others, it shall be done unto you. We reap what we sow, and if you thrive on exposing or gossiping or magnifying the short comings of others, there will come a day that if you ever come short in any area that someone will do the same thing to you. So again I say, we don't encourage condone, but what we do encourage is cover, pray, seek God, intercede for that leader and we must learn to be restorers, learn to restore leaders.

A man or woman with a right spirit will submit themselves to God and then to the congregation they will sit themselves down. If they don't sit themselves down and you feel that you can't remain under that covering, then leave with prayerful direction. Let us be careful what we speak out of our mouth and what we say. Let us adopt Uriah's persuasion and also the character of Noah's sons. We don't agree with your sin, we don't like what you have done. What you have done is biblically and morally wrong, but we love God enough and love you enough that we will cover you until you get victory and or deliverance in the area of your struggle. We must keep in mind also, that according to Jeremiah, if the shepherd is smitten, then the flock is scattered. Let us not be selfish in our ambition, anxious to reveal or expose. Saints not only are we accountable to God for ourselves, but we are accountable to God for others. Consider the effect that it has on the sheep of the church.

Yes, I admit that there are many leaders who are

not living what they preach, that are not in right relationship with God. There are some who are genuinely struggling trying to overcome struggle, stronghold, sin, and through Christ, they will. If they seek the face of the Lord, deny their flesh through fasting and prayer and get under the right covering, teaching and counsel. Many times God does not openly or readily expose leaders that are in error, not because He favors them over the laity, but because God knows great would be the fall of the people. In being sensitive, we must understand the devastating affect that disgrace and reproach has on the membership of any church when they discover that the character, the integrity, or the lifestyle of the leader is not in compliance with the word of God. Not only does it affect you, the individual, but it greatly affects the leadership or the membership. Let us keep this in mind and consider the heart of the sheep.

Proverbs, Chapter 6 gives us to know that there are six abominable sins and the one that God hates the most is "he that sows discord among the brethren." Discord means you bring dissension, schisms, confusion, separation, causing the church to fall out, breakup, the saints of God to be at odds with each other. Saints, even if what you perceive is factual and you know it to be factual, I ask you the question that Paul asks the Roman church in Romans, Chapter 14 when he dealt with the liberty of the believer. He said, *Walketh thou not charitably."* In other words, don't you walk in love. Paul said something very profound, he said I will not be a stumbling block or an offense to my brother for whom Christ died. Therefore, if eating meat causeth my brother to stumble or be offended, I won't eat it. In other words, even gossiping or spending news be it true or false, if that is going to cause somebody to stumble or be offended, then Paul said don't you walk in enough love, in enough maturity not to do it. Not for the sake of covering someone but for the sake of being sensitive or concerned about souls.

The words of God also declares this in the book of Proverbs, that a faithful man concealeth a matter but a talebearer revealeth secrets. Talebearer means a busy body, a gossiper, one of the most detestable things the word of God speaks about is when Paul wrote to Titus admonishing him to tell the women not to be busy bodies in other men's matters. I again reemphasize Proverbs 11:13, it says, *"A talebearer revealeth secrets: but he that is of a faithful spirit concealeth the matter."* Again, that does not imply that you cover or rather condone sin. The translation of the Hebrew word is holechrachil and it means this, a walking busy body, a peddler in scandal.

As a matter of fact as we reference this in Leviticus 19:6 and also in the New Testament James 1:20, it refers to he who reveals whatever is confided to him. He will even reveal his own secrets rather than to have nothing to say at all. And that's very scary, to be willing to tell his own business or reveal his own secrets. The word of God confirms the same scripture in Proverbs 20:19, it says, *"He that goeth about as a talebearer revealeth secrets: therefore meddle not with him that flattereth with his lips."* In other words the commentary says don't even have fellowship, don't conversate with him.

Keep this in mind, that God will never promote you in the kingdom if He can't trust you. Throughout the scripture, we read He reveals His secrets to His servants and not just the revealing of God's secrets but things that have been revealed to you by flesh entities. You will never be a faithful leader if you have not learned to be confidential. We in the kingdom make commitments and take vows, such as attorneys, they have something called an attorney-client confidentiality clause and privilege. In other words, no matter what that client tells the attorney, a defendant can tell the attorney that he committed the crime but the attorney is obligated by law, in confidentiality, to keep that between him and the individual, defendant, or the accused that told min.

Don't let it be named among you, that you are a busy body, a gossiper. If you can't be trusted with the secrets of men, how can God trust you with the secrets and the deep things of the kingdom of God? Don't be a busybody, don't be a talebearer, don't be a reciprocal to carry junk and trash, because it only reflects on you in the end.

Chapter 8

TOUCH NOT MY ANOINTED

⚜

For reference, we are going to the book of I Chronicles 16:14-22, it reads, *"He is the LORD our God; his judgments are in all the earth."* Verse 15, *"Be ye mindful always of his covenant; the word which he commanded to a thousand generations;"* Verse 16, *"Even of the covenant which he made with Abraham, and of his oath unto Isaac;"* Verse 17, *"And hath confirmed the same to Jacob for a law and to Israel for an everlasting covenant,"* Verse 18, *"Saying Unto thee will I give the land of Canaan, the lot of your inheritance;"* Verse 19, *"When ye were but few, even a few, and strangers in it."* Verse 20, *"And when they went from nation to nation, and from one kingdom to another people;"* Verse 21, *"He suffered no man to do them wrong: yea, he reproved kings for their sakes,"* Verse 22, *"Saying, Touch not mine anointed, and do my prophets no harm."*

Again, I reiterate the title of this chapter, "Touch Not My Anointed." In this scripture text it refers to the Abrahamic covenant, the covenant that God made with Abraham. Notice the seriousness of God as it relates to His covenant or relationship with His chosen men and women. Here He is reaffirming to the people, be mindful always of His covenant. In other words, if God made a covenant with you, God is not slack concerning His promise that some men count slackness as I Peter 3:9 says, if God said it, He is going to bring it to pass.

Numbers 23:19 says, *"God is not a man, that he should lie; neither the son of man, that he should repent: hath he said, and shall he not do it? Or hath he spoken, and shall he not make it good?"* So God is faithful to His word, He watches over His word to perform it, which literally means, He baby-sits His word, like a nurse does a baby, nurses His word to make sure it performs what He sent it to do. Isaiah 59 said, *"that the word will not come back unto us void, but it will accomplish the thing it was sent to do."*

In other words, the word can't come back without a testimony or without a report. So it is with a covenant. If God has established a covenant with you, he is faithful to His covenant and He is going to watch over it to make sure that it comes to pass.

One of my favorite scriptures in the book of Titus, Chapter 1:2 says, *"In hope of eternal life, which God, that cannot lie, promised."* The word promised is a Greek word 'huper tomazai' and it means announced. God, who cannot lie announced, He spoke into the heavens, He spoke into the earth, He spoke under the earth, He spoke to hell, He spoke to the demonic posers and entities, principalities, and the rulers of the darkness of this age, He spoke, He announced that His purpose would be accomplished in the earth and that His word and His thoughts concerning you would be completed. In reference to covenant, in I Chronicles 16:16 it says, *"Even of the covenant which he made with Abraham, and of his oath unto Isaac.* Verse 17, *"And hath confirmed the same to Jacob for a law, and to Israel for an everlasting covenant."*

Now what you must understand is that when this covenant was established there was nobody but Abraham in this covenant. It was a period for about twenty-five years Abraham was the only party in the covenant, then for sixty years there was only Abraham and Isaac. Then for the next seventy to eighty years there was only Abraham, Isaac and Jacob, then came the twelve sons of Jacob and their families, seventy people total when Jacob went into Egypt. This was exactly 215 years of the 450 years that is spoken of.

Now what we must understand is, that God is faithful to His word, but let us see how serious He is about His covenant. Even though it took all these years, He said in verse 18, *"Saying, Unto thee will I give the land of Canaan, the lot of your inheritance;"* Verse 19, *"When ye were but few, even a few, and strangers in it.".* The Lord said when it was just a few of you I promised you I would bring you into a wealthy place. And when they went from nation to nation referring to Abraham, Isaac and Jacob and from one kingdom to another people, He suffered with no man to do them wrong. In other words God would not allow the enemy to prevail against them.

Why? Because God is faithful to His covenant. He is faithful to His word. If we abide in Him as John said in St. John, *"And his word abide in us."* We can ask what we will, not only that, remember the promise of Psalms 9:1, *"He that dwelleth in the secret places of the most High shall abide under the shadow of the almighty."* His anointed is not just in His presence, but were under His shadow. And I Chronicles 16:21 says, *"He suffered no man to do them wrong: yea, he reproved kings for their sakes."* Can you imagine that, that God is so in love with you and His covenant is so serious that He would reprove, that means arrest. Bring to a halt, correct, shut down, make inoperable, kings for your sake. That's how much He honors covenant. Verse 22, *"Saying, Touch not mine anointed, and do my prophets no harm."*

The reason I feel it is of great necessity that I share this with you, is because we must understand our position in Christ. We are hid in Christ with God. And understand that God takes covenant relationship very, very, very seriously. Anytime He would reprove a king and shut down nations and overturn decisions for the sake of those that are anointed, those that are in covenant with Him, then we should revere and honor the covenant that establishes first of all with us and then with men and women of God. So we must be careful how we handle and how we entreat the anointing.

In the book of Esther we read in Chapter 4 a very

profound scripture. As I look in Esther this is very thought provoking and very challenging to see how serious God takes covenant, how serious He takes His anointing and that He does not make light of anyone offending His anointed. You remember the words of Jesus, *"It is better to put a millstone around your neck and jump into a lake then to offend one of his little ones."* In other words, it is better to commit suicide then to mess with one of my anointed.

In the book of Esther, Chapter 4:10 it says, *"Again Esther spake unto Hatach, and gave him commandment unto Mordecai;"* Verse 11, *"All the king's servants, and the people of the king's provinces, do know, that whosoever, whether man or woman, shall come unto the king into the inner court, who is not called, there is one law of his to put him to death, except such to whom the king shall hold out the golden sceptre, that he may live: but I have not been called to come in unto the king these thirty days."* And this is Hatach and the servants reminding Esther that she could not go to the king unannounced, because if men could just walk up to the anointing with a complaint, with a murmur, with an accusation, or a charge immediately you would be put to death, except the king held out the gold scepter.

Now again, and I reiterate this, we are not teaching man worship, neither are we coveting the sin of emulation for you to esteem the man more than creator, but we must recognize the seriousness of God's covenant with men and women that He has placed in leadership. Also we must see how serious God takes it when we offend one of little ones.

It was known that if you approached the king or any man or woman in leadership unannounced it was worthy of a death sentence. We must be very careful of how we confront and approach the anointing or the anointed ones. Why? Because they belong to God. They are God's chosen vessels. They are those who the Lord has appointed and divinely placed in the areas of leadership and ministry that He wants them to walk in. So it behooves us to be extra careful and very mindful of what we say and how we say it; of how we confront, how we approach even if there is concern. We should do it in the spirit of meekness, but also in respect, not worshipping the man but honoring the God in the man or the God in the woman.

Again, I say, that if God seriously thought enough of leadership of men and women, that are anointed or specifically called for certain anointing, ministries and offices, that He would say if you approach in the wrong way that it could be detrimental, then I think that we should take to heart the word of the Lord. No, preachers are not God's, no they are not infallible, they are flesh like you and I. They have short comings and struggles and make mistakes like we do. But we must recognize that we have to be careful how we approach and how handle the anointing and the anointed.

Chapter 9

WHO MINISTERS TO THE MINISTER?

-❈-

In the previous chapter, I shared with you the importance of how we approach the anointing. This may invoke or arouse the curiosity. You may ask, "Well then, Pastor Dash, who has a right to confront leadership, who has a right to reprove them, correct them, bring them in check?"

God has always anointed particular and specific men and women to minister to leaders. We should never take it upon ourselves, unless God has placed us in an office or an anointing, where He has called us to go to the prophet or to the prophetess, to the leader, to the man or the woman of God. If you are anointed to do so you will know it. God will let you know and not only that, but the leader will know because he will receive your word. But even in reprove or speaking the truth in love, we never approach them in arrogance. We never go in self will or self centered, but we move by the leading of the Lord.

When David, in the book of Samuel, sinned, took Bathsheba from Uriah the Hittite and slept with her and sinned, the prophet Nathan came to David and told David a little story about a man who stole two little ewe lambs from a poor person. When David heard this, the word of God said that he became very angry and wroth in his spirit and David said, "I command that this man wrought recompense and restore double or two-fold what he stole." David asked the question, "Who is this man?" The prophet Nathan spoke back to David and said, "Thou art the man."

Now David could have done one of two things. He could have become arrogant and said, "Get out of my presence, Nathan, who do you think you are talking to. I am the king," or he could have humbled himself like he did and repented and asked God to forgive him and pleaded for mercy. But Nathan was the prophet assigned to the king. Everyone that is in ministry is not necessarily the prophet that is assigned to the priest of the house.

God will reveal to you by His spirit, not only by His spirit, but He will put it in the heart of the leader. If you are in a local assembly, they will come to you before you go to them. They will come to you in confidence seeking either your opinion, counsel, guidance or just for you to be in agreement with them about some issues. So who ministers to the minister? Those men and women that God have anointed the spirit of wisdom and counsel, those that are seasoned in the Lord, those that are learned, those that are mature in the Lord. So who ministers to the minister? Those that God will anoint to do so.

You may ask, "Well what do you do when leaders hurt, who helps heal the hurting? As Paul spoke in II Corinthians Chapter 1, where he was so discouraged and so depressed that he despaired even life. He didn't want to live, he got so discouraged that he was ready to die, but then he understood his purpose. The spirit of the Lord refreshed Paul and ministered to his hurt and he began to write to others and told them in Philippians, Chapter 1, *"that now I understand everything that has happened unto me has happened for the furtherance of the gospel."* But the Lord had people strategically placed to minister to Paul.

Understand that the leaders are human, they hurt like you do. Just like when Elijah fled Jezebel and ran and hid under the Juniper tree. But notice what the word of God said in I Kings, Chapter 17, Elijah get up from that Juniper tree, he sent the raven to feed him. But listen to what the word of God said, I Kings 17:9, *"Arise, get thee to Zarepath, which belongeth to Zidon, and dwell there: behold, I have commanded a widow woman there to sustain thee."* In other words, God said, "I have already put somebody in place to minister to you." You will know when God has placed someone in position to minister to you. You will know when god has placed someone in position to minister to the leader.

What do you do Bishop Dash when leaders fall, like when David fell? God raised up a Nathan. Well how do you tell leaders that they are tired, they are burnt out, they need to sit back, they need to go away and be refreshed? Moses experienced that. The Bible says that Moses heard the cry of the people and their complaints from sun up to sun down. Imagine one man with possibly a million or more people following his congregation, but the Lord raised up Jethro, Moses' father-in-law, and he said, "Moses this is too much for you. You can't lead the people, and counsel them individually." He said, "Appoint elders over different groups and tribes, appoint seventy elders, some by hundreds, some by fifties, some by thousands." God used Jethro to speak wisdom to Moses, he encouraged Moses, and told Moses you can't do it all by yourself. You need the help and the counsel of these other brethren.

God never anointed one man or one woman to do everything. That's why I encourage you, who read this, particularly those of you who are ministers of the gospel, you that are intercessors, you that are armor bearers, get in your place, get in position. The Lord has divinely connected you with ministry so that you could help carry the burden, help carry the vision, help minister to the needs of the people. No matter how anointed a man or a woman is, they still need other anointed men and women to help carry out the mandate and the mission of God. So in order to avoid burn out make sure that there is counsel. All of us need to be accountable to someone, (Moses has a Jethro, and the Lord will take care of that) make sure that you are in your place, make sure that you are the Aaron and the Hur, that whenever the leaders arms got weary you were there to hold them up. Remember it is important to keep his or her arms held up because as long as their arms are up, you prevail, the church wins, we overcome. When they get weary and their arms drop that's when we start to lose as it was with Moses and the children of Israel.

Some may ask again, "What about leadership Bishop Dash and accountability, how do we deal with leadership and accountability?" Leadership and accountability, every leader is accountable to God. Someone may ask, should they not be accountable to man, yes they should. If you remember the story of Saul when Saul was made king, not by the choice of God, but by the choice of the people. Even after Saul had displeased the Lord and began to operate and move in his own flesh and lost his anointing and got out of the will of God. There is still a degree, a certain level accountability, for the Lord often would send the prophet Samuel to speak to Saul. If he would only have heeded the counsel and humbled himself, perhaps God would have spared him and he would have maintained his anointing even though he wasn't the choice of God.

So in all, sensitivity first to God because we cannot be sensitive or discerning or fill anyone if we are not first sensitive to God. The infamous cliché says, "Before we can talk to men about God, we must first talk to God about men, so that God by way of the Holy Spirit may make us sensitive to them and sensitive to their needs." So that you can properly and adequately minister to them, not according to our flesh because there are times that you may not feel like doing that, but by the leading of the spirit of God.

In so much that we are not governed by our

emotion, sometimes you may be in disagreement, total disagreement with a leader. You may be in total disagreement with a man or woman of God, but it is so very important my friend that we be careful as to how we conduct ourselves, in what we do and how we present our self. So who ministers to the minister, again I refer to I Kings, Chapter 17, when thethe Lord said, *"I have already commanded a widow woman there to sustain thee."* God will strategically put men and women in place to minister to the needs of those that he has placed in the fore front, in the headship, in the leadership.

Chapter 10

THE SPIRIT OF THE FORE-RUNNER

⊷≍⊶

A fore-runner is a person that goes before the leader, the speaker. They are deemed as the announcer, the preparer one that prepares the way. In the gospel according to Matthew, we read about the birth of Jesus Christ and the word of God speaks of His birth. Prior to the birth of Jesus, we read about Elizabeth the mother of John and Mary who is the mother of Jesus. The story is told that when Elizabeth shared the good news with Mary that she had conceived and her and her husband Zacharias were in awe of the conception.

You know the story, Elizabeth was barren, not able to conceive and the angel of the Lord visited Zacharias and spoke to him about the conception of his wife and the news was so wonderful, the joy was so great that literally when Mary shared the news that she was with Jesus the word of God says that the joy was so great that John literally leaped in the belly of Elizabeth. The word of God reads in the gospel according to Matthew 1:18 reads, *"Now the birth of Jesus Christ was on this wise: When as his mother Mary was espoused to Joseph, before they came together, she was found with child of the Holy Ghost."* Verse 19, *"Then Joseph her husband, being a just man, and not willing to make her a publick example, was minded to put her away privily."*

In other words, it was unheard of for someone to be impregnated by the Holy Spirit. Joseph being a fair man said, "I won't expose you openly, I will put you away or separate myself from you, but I'll do it in secret." Verse 20, *"But while he thought on these things, behold, the angle of the Lord appeared unto him in a dream, saying, Joseph, thou son of David, fear not to take unto thee Mary thy wife: for that which is conceived in her is of the Holy Ghost."* The angel calmed his fears, his apprehension and said, "Don't be afraid, for that which is in her is of the Holy Ghost." Verse 21, *"And she shall bring forth a son, and thou shalt call his name JESUS: for he shall save his people from their sins."* Verse 22, *"Now all this was done, that it might be fulfilled which was spoken of the Lord by the prophet, saying,"* Verse 23, *"Behold, a virgin shall be with child, and shall bring forth a son, and they shall call his name Emmanuel, which being interpreted is God with us."* Verse 24, *"Then Joseph being raised from sleep did as the angel of the Lord had bidden him, and took unto him his wife:"* Verse 25, *"And knew her not till she had brought forth her firstborn son:*

and he called his name Jesus." Joseph reverenced the word of the Lord from the angel so much that even after they were married he would not consummate their marriage, nor would he come together with his wife until after it had been confirmed and the Christ child had been born.

So we see the miraculous set up of God, we see divine intervention. God will always raise up strategically and place someone to prepare the way.

A fore-runner operates in many different capacities. They prepared the way for the man or woman of God in the book of Acts. The early church often sent ministry workers before them to intercede, discern, spy out the land, publicize, or announce what was forth coming. Gehazi was messenger and fore-runner to Elijah in the book of Kings. It is very important that you understand your calling. If the Lord has called you to walk with your leader, out of the hundreds of thousands of believers in your region. God could have chosen anyone, but he chose you. Therefore walk circumspectly. Don't be a busy body in other men's matters. Live a blameless life without reproach, operate in wisdom, be filled with the Holy Ghost, have a good report, ask the Lord to teach you how to properly intercede, expect opposition, jealousy and envy. Remember you were not voted into your office, but divinely appointed. Two vital things to keep even before you posture and position. You like Elijah, may feel unworthy or unfit, I Kings 19:19. Elijah was a farmer plowing in the field like Amos, who said, "I'm not a prophet nor the son of a prophet, but just a keeper of the

Sycamore tree." In other words, I'm just a vine dresser. Amos 7:14.

Let's address posture being aligned with vision anointing. Many in the body of Christ miss God's choicest blessing because they are out of place at the decree. Being in the right place at the right time is very significant. Timing is essential to blessing in II Kings 2. Posture is projected in verse 9. Elijah said to Elisha, "Ask what you want." Had Elisha not maintained alignment with his mentor, he would have missed the anointing of transference.

Paul admonished Timothy by saying *"Store up the gift of God in you which was given."* Timothy 1:6 *"to you by laying on of my hands.*

Your leader has a deposit of transference in them for you. This is proven again when Paul said, *"For I long to see you, that I may impart unto you some spiritual gift, to the end ye may be established:"* Romans 1:11. The Greek word 'established,' es-stable-ment (GR steroidzo) means to be strengthened, anointed, above the norm. It comes from the English word steroid.

Going back to II Kings 2:9, Elisha asked Elijah for a double portion of his spirit, Elijah's response was "You have asked a hard thing. The Hebrew word 'hard' is 'quashah' which means hard labor or difficult, almost impossible thing. The commentary says, Elijah's question you twice as much as I have, but, according to record, it came to pass. Elijah experienced 16 miracles and Elisha experienced 32 miracles for reference of the double anointing. James 5:17 Elijah shut up the heavens for three and a half years, II Kings 8:1 clearly states Elisha shut up the heavens for seven years double the time frame.

Elijah's request II Kings 2:10, "If thou see me when I'm taken from you." In other words if you are in position when I'm elevated, it shall be so unto you. The mantle will fall on you.

A nugget to every believer, never become insecure or intimidated when new members or new converts come to your local assembly. It only means God wants to promote you. That's when discipleship comes into operation. You train them to assume your position so that the pastor can elevate you to a higher ministry position and calling. Elijah had to move up so that Elisha could move in.

The latter clause of II Kings 2:10, *"but if not, it shall not be so."* If you are not accountable, faithful, diligent, visible and dependable how then shall you expect to receive promotion. *"Promotion cometh not from the east or west, but promotion cometh from the lord,"* Psalm 75:6.

"Humble yourselves therefore under the mighty hand of God, that he may exalt you in due time:" I Peter 5:6.

"God is a Spirit," John 4:24. He does not have a physical hand. The scripture that alludes to God's hand refer to his authority. The hand of God is the five-fold gifting and governing of the church. Ephesians 4:11. Thumb, Apostle—foundation; Prophet—pointer, direction, Pastor; Middle finger—balance, evangelist; Fourth finger—teacher; fifth finger –guide counsel.

Back to II Kings, if you see me the carrier, leaders are carriers, agents representatives. You must have tunnel vision, locked on the anointing and the anointed, not to overemphasize, the man, but everything God did in the earth He did it through a man or woman.

God is a God of relationship and covenant, thus it is very important to maintain a good report with the oracle that has been predestined to develop your purpose and destiny. In Numbers 12:1-9, Aaron, who was Moses fore-runner said *"Hath the Lord spoken only by Moses?"* In other words, does not God speak to anyone else? The response is Yes, God does, however there is certain dialogue between God and senior centership and mysteries of the kingdom that he only reveals to the prophets. He revealeth his secrets to his servants, the prophets.

God said, "Any other senior leader I'll speak to in visions or dreams, but with Moses I'll speak mouth to mouth." Your Moses/Pastor, Prophet, Bishop, Apostle goes to God on your behalf, Romans 13 says, *"Rulers are not a terror to good works, but to evil."* The criteria for being an effective forerunner is not your intelligence, gifting, influence alone, but rather your faithfulness. I Corinthians 4:2 says, *"It is required in stewards,"* (one responsible for handling the things of God.) *"that a man be found faithful."*

I pray that the eyes of your understanding be enlightened, as you walk in the principles of the Elisha Concept.

Remember II Kings 2:10, *"If you see me when*

I'm taken from thee," (elevation-promotion) *"it shall be unto thee."*

In service for the King (Christ)

Vance L. Dash, Sr.

NOTES

Other Publications by Bishop Vance L Dash, Sr.

The Elijah Principle—Leadership & Covenant

Strategies of Warfare—Levels of Demonic Attack

Destiny Is Calling You—Origin & Destination

Aren't You Better Than the Birds—God's Provision

Ish & Isha—Man-Woman Relationships

The Overflow—About Praise & Worship

Breaking Generational Curses—Course through Genetics

Many others forthcoming, such as:
Prophetic Dimensions
And many more..........

For Further Information please contact:
 Rhema Deliverance Center
 3527-29 N. Smedley St.
 Philadelphia, PA 19140
 Phone: (215) 225-9650
 Fax: (215) 225-9625
 Web Site: INFO@RDCENTER.ORG

Printed in the United States
22348LVS00001B/106-276

9 781594 676215